ENDTIME PROPHECIES AMPLIFIED

ENDTIME PROPHECIES AMPLIFIED

DAVID D. CEIGA

Kravitz & Sons

INNOVATORS IN PUBLISHING, MARKETING AND ADVERTISING

Kravitz and Sons LLC
1301 Farmville Blvd, Suite 104
Greenville, NC 27834

Published by Kravitz and Sons LLC.

ISBN: 979-8-89639-230-9 (sc)
ISBN: 979-8-89639-231-6 (e)

Library of Congress Control Number: 2025905970

CONTENTS

AUTHOR'S INTRODUCTION

AMOS WAS ONLY a farmer, an unqualified prophet according to the world's standard. Yet God told him to go and he went, and confronted by Amaizah the priest during the reign of king Jeroboam's in Israel. Amos was accused by the king as being God's messenger, because he did not want to hear what needed to be said. Amos responded to Amaziah by saying, "*I was no prophet, neither was I a prophet's son; but I was a herdsman, and a gatherer of sycamore fruit: And the Lord took me as I followed the flock, and the Lord said to me, Go, prophesy to My people Israel*" (**Amos 7:14-15**).

I suppose we could also say that I am not a pastor or one with theologian credentials, either. We can say the same thing for all of the first century Christians as well. Most of them were simple fishermen, farmers, tax collectors and tent makers; with the exception of Paul who was a Pharisee. Sometimes God will just say "Go", and not wait for a second opinion, approval from others or some completing of a degree to assure the qualification. Don't get me wrong, education is great and very important. But when it comes to the things of God, we don't qualify ourselves; God qualifies us. God sees and knows our hearts, and that is all He needs. He also knows our desires and potential within us. Wherever we are at in the moment we are called to do something bigger than ourselves; to be sent.

I spent sixteen years in the military and fourteen years in a factory plus other blue collar jobs since the age of thirteen. I have helped several people with social and personal problems. At the same time I am not perfect, I have missed the mark more times then I care to remember. I can safely say that our jobs or careers have nothing to do with our full potential in life. We all have some type of skill or trade that guides us to our main purpose. It is through these experiences that draws us to our destiny. I'm just someone that hungers for truth;

some learned through years of experiences and others through years of research and studies. I have studied several subject topics regarding the bible. Bible prophecies have been by far the most consuming. After reviewing the information and the evidence from well-known authors and scholars in their fields, through the years, I have compiled this book, with nuggets for you to think about. Which, I have never ever attempted to put a book together, until now.

I have used Bible scriptures as the main foundation along with some historical facts and the current events facing our world today. I will share various viewpoints I've uncovered in my research, some I agree with, while others I don't. I will explain both sides either way, the whys, then let you decide. My main focus for this book is to be different from all the other ideologies. I will try to keep this book as short as possible and easy to read and understand. You may not be an expert; neither am I. But we can still read the readable "Signs" or things that God has given us in order to know what is going on around us. God makes all things possible for our understanding. To fully understand endtime prophecy, know that they don't necessarily just happen to go by the numbers or some alphabetical, chronological order. Sometimes the Bible tells us the order of sequence, other times we can make sense of how the orders may follow, as per historical evidence or facts with present current events. As for the Seals, Trumpets and Vials; the Bible seems to be clear to their order.

Everything else in the book of Revelation seems a bit chaotic. Know the pattern! In the Old as well as the New Testament they bounce back and forth as they mesh together. Sometimes it's as simple as getting back to the basics. God wants us to know these things or He would have never given us so many hints. Over one third of the whole Bible is given to prophecies so it is important and clear that we should be mindful as they come to pass and what will follow in the days coming. What is forming in the world around us will shock you. Search and find the truth for yourself. I prefer the old normal (ways, the things of God); there is a new normal heading our way. Paul has warned us in **Romans 12:2,** *not to conform to the world's standards, but to be transformed by the renewing of our minds.*

A few points I need to make in dealing with Biblical Prophecies, before we get started. God does not make any errors or mistakes. I know what you're thinking; duh, no kidding. You would be amazed at how so many people try to cram and force these puzzle pieces to fit their own narratives and ideas. Even though they probably mean well. So the errors and mistakes came from our end not God's. We try to redefine the Bible to our own liking, instead of allowing the Bible to define us. God is very organized, detailed, direct and precise, in what He has written. What He has said can refer to different types or meaning of things when we are dealing with our struggles. This is why we can read through the Bible several times and still continue to learn and apply something into our everyday life. Theologians say that this is why the Words in the Bible come alive, in a Spiritual sense; this is where the Bible never gets old but always stays refreshed. So the Bible is different than any other book ever written on the planet.

The animals in Daniel 7 are the same as in Revelation chapter 13! Also, the serpent in Genesis chapter three means the same as the serpent in the book of Revelation. What means one thing in one book means the same in the other book as long as the subject is the same, without losing its original content. God is a God of order. Remember, with the exception of Apollo and Paul, the first century followers of Christ turn the known world of their day upside down. They were uneducated outcasts and held low economic status. Everything has a purpose and a reason. We cannot shape and mold God into our purpose as God shapes and molds us into His purpose. The truth will always remain the truth, and a lie will always be a lie. I will share some nuggets and then move on. I do hope you do your own research and study for the truth. God Bless You!

1. God uses symbolism that the people of those days (or Bible times) were familiar with.

2. God uses the nature of the animal to represent the nature of the nation or kingdom it will represent (or match). I will explain this later in the book.

3. God wants us to search out the scriptures for theses interpretation.

4. Symbolism can also hide the meaning and protect the writer like John and symbol itself, such as a kingdom or nation.

5. God is a Spiritual Being (Heavenly Father) that authored a Spiritual Book, for and to Spiritual beings (mankind).

I give special thanks to my wife, Sara for putting up with me and loving me so much through our ups and downs of 40 plus years of marriage. I truly value her inputs, and pushing me to make this book even possible and in which this book may not have even became a reality. She has always believed in me and I thank her and love her so much. She has been my driving force.

I also would like to thank my parents: my step father Frank Ross (1941-2018) and my mother Yolanda Ross (1938-2022). I have learned so much from the lives they lived and the people they have touched. Together that made me the man I am today.

CHAPTER ONE

JESUS' FORETOLD EVENTS

FIRST THINGS FIRST, I would like to start and add the words that Jesus Christ Himself spoke regarding these End Time signs. I feel it is very important for our understanding and clarity. As you read these words of Jesus, keep in mind who He was talking to. The conversations Jesus was having were not with the multitudes or crowds of people but a small inner group of select individuals known as His disciples; the "Church" people after Christ's resurrection. These same disciples would birth the "Church Age" after His resurrection and ascension. He also gave them the tools they would need, the Baptism of the Holy Spirit at Pentecost. He never told them not to worry because this would never happen to them or us. On the contrary it can and will affect everyone on this planet and the things in it. He does have a way of divinely protecting His faithful believers. Also keep in mind that Satan also has his own wrath, curses, and persecution towards God's chosen people. Stay focus and stay the course, God will go with and be with you until the End.

(Matthew 10:16-42, AMP). *Behold, I am sending you out like sheep in the midst of wolves; be wary and wise as serpents, and be innocent (harmless, guileless, and without falsity) as doves. Be on guard against men [whose way or nature is to act in opposition to God]; for they will deliver you up to councils and flog you in their synagogues (churches and legal systems), and you will be brought before governors and kings for <u>My sake,</u> as a <u>witness</u> to bear <u>testimony</u> before them and to the Gentiles (the nations). But when they deliver you up, <u>do not be anxious</u> about how or what you are to speak; for what you are to say will be given you in that very hour and moment, for it is not you who are speaking, but the Spirit of your Father speaking through you. Brother <u>will deliver</u> up brother <u>to death,</u> and the father his child; and children will take a <u>stand against</u> their parents and will have them <u>put to death.</u> And you <u>will be hated</u> by all for My name's sake, but he who <u>perseveres</u> and <u>endures</u> to the end will be saved [from spiritual disease and death in the world to come]. When they persecute you in one town [that is, pursue you in a manner that would injure you and cause you to suffer because of your belief], <u>flee</u> to another town; for truly I tell you, you will not have gone through all the towns of Israel before the Son of Man comes. A disciple is not above his teacher, nor is a servant or slave above his master. It is sufficient for the disciple to be like his teacher, and the servant or slave like his master. If they have called the Master of the house Beelzebub [master of the dwelling], how much more will they speak evil of those of His household. So <u>have no fear</u> of them; for nothing is concealed that will not be revealed, or kept secret that will not become known. What I say to you in the dark, tell in the light; and what you hear whispered in the ear, proclaim upon the housetops. And <u>do not be afraid</u> of those who kill the body but cannot kill the soul; but rather be afraid of Him who can destroy both soul and body in hell (Gehenna). Are not two little sparrows sold for a penny? And yet not one of them will fall to the ground without your Father's leave (consent) and notice. But even the very hairs of your head are all numbered. <u>Fear Not,</u> then; you are of more value than many sparrows. Therefore, everyone who* *acknowledge Me before men and confesses Me [out of a state of oneness with Me], I will also acknowledge him before My Father Who is in heaven and confess [that I am abiding in] him. But whoever denies and disowns Me before men, I also will deny and disown him before My Father Who is in heaven. Do not think that I have come to bring peace upon the earth; I have not come to bring peace, but a sword. For I have come to part asunder a man from his father, and a daughter from her mother, and a newly married wife from her mother-in-law. And a man's foes will be they of his own household. He who loves [and takes more pleasure in] father and mother more than [in] Me is not worthy of Me; and he who loves [and takes more pleasure in] son or daughter more than [in] Me is not worthy of Me; And he who does not take up his cross and follow Me [cleave steadfastly to Me, conforming wholly to My example in living and, if need be, in dying also] is not worthy of Me. Whoever finds his [lower] life will lose it [the higher life], and whoever loses his [lower] life on My account will find it [the higher life]. He who receives and welcomes and accepts you receives and welcomes and accepts Me, and he who receives and welcomes and accepts Him Who sent Me. He who receives and welcomes and accepts a prophet because he is a prophet shall receive a prophet's reward, and he who receives and welcomes and accepts a righteous man because he is a righteous man shall receive a righteous man's reward. And whoever gives to one of these little ones [in rank or influence] even a cup of cold water because he is My disciple, surely I declare to you, he shall not lose his reward.*

Even though He was first speaking to His original disciples, prior to sending them out **(10:5-15)**, as Jesus continued, change occurred as He started focusing on all the futuristic disciples and believers. There are no other accounts mentioning this in great details.

(Matthew 24:4-44 NCV). *Jesus answered, Be careful that no one fools you. Many will come in my name, saying, 'I am the Christ,' and they will fool many people. You will hear about wars and stories of wars that are coming, but don't be afraid. These things must happen before the end comes. Nations will fight against other* *nations; kingdoms will fight against other kingdoms. There will be times when there is <u>no food</u> for people to eat, and there will be <u>earthquakes</u> in different places. These things are like the <u>first pains when something new is about to be born.</u> Then people will <u>arrest</u> you, hand you over to be <u>hurt,</u> and <u>kill</u> you. They will <u>hate you</u> because you believe in me. At that time, <u>many will lose their faith,</u> and they will <u>turn against each other</u> and <u>hate each other.</u> Many <u>false prophets</u> will come and cause many people to <u>believe lies.</u> There will be more and <u>more evil in the world,</u> so most people will <u>stop showing their love</u> for each other. But those people who <u>keep their faith</u> until the end will be saved. The Good News about God's kingdom will be preached in all the world, to every nation. Then the end will come. Daniel the prophet spoke about 'the destroying terror.' You will see this standing in the holy place. (You who read this should understand what it means.) At that time, the people in Judea should <u>run away</u> to the mountains. If people are on the roofs of their houses, they must not go down to get anything out of their houses. If people are in the fields, they must not go back to get their coats. At that time, how <u>terrible</u> it will be for women who are pregnant or have nursing babies! Pray that it will not be winter or a Sabbath day when these things happen and you have to run away, because at that time there will be <u>much trouble.</u> There will be <u>more trouble</u> than there has ever been since the beginning of the world until now, and nothing as bad will ever happen again. God has decided to make that <u>terrible time short.</u> Otherwise, no one would go on living. But God will make that time short to help the people he has chosen. At that time, someone might say to you, 'Look, there is the Christ!' Or another person might say, 'There he is!' But don't believe them. <u>False Christs</u> and <u>false prophets</u> will come and perform great <u>wonders</u> and <u>miracles.</u> They will try <u>to fool</u> even the people God has chosen, if that is possible. Now I have warned you about this before it happens. If people tell you, 'The Christ is in the desert,' don't go there. If they say, 'The Christ is in the inner room,' <u>don't believe</u> it. When the Son of Man comes, he will be seen by everyone, like lightning flashing from the east to the west. Wherever the dead body is, there the vultures will gather. Soon <u>after the trouble</u> of those days, 'the <u>sun will grow dark,</u> and the <u>moon will not give its light.</u> The <u>stars will fall</u> from the sky. And the powers* *of the heavens will be shaken.' At that time, the sign of the Son of Man will appear in the sky. Then all the peoples of the world will cry. They will see the Son of Man coming on clouds in the sky with great power and glory. He will use a loud trumpet to send his angels all around the earth, and they will gather his chosen people from every part of the world. Learn a lesson from the fig tree: When its branches become green and soft and new leaves appear, you know summer is near. In the same way, when you see all these things happening, you will know that the time is near, ready to come. I tell you the truth, all these things will happen while the people of this time are still living. Earth and sky will be destroyed, but the words I have said will never be destroyed. No one knows when that day or time will be, not the angels in heaven, not even the Son. Only the Father knows. When the Son of Man comes, it will be like what happened during Noah's time. In those days before the flood, people were eating and drinking, marrying and giving their children to be married, until the day Noah entered the boat. They knew nothing about what was happening until the flood came and destroyed them. It will be the same when the Son of Man comes. Two men will be in the field. One will be taken, and the other will be left. Two women will be grinding grain with a mill. One will be taken, and the other will be left. So always be ready, because you don't know the day your Lord will come. Remember owner would watch and not let the thief break in. So you also must be ready, because the Son of Man will come at a time you don't expect him.*

(Mark 13:5-33 HCSB). *Then Jesus began by telling them: Watch out that no one deceives you. Many will come in My name, saying, I am He,' and they will deceive many. When you hear of wars and rumors of wars, don't be alarmed; these things must take place, but the end is not yet. For nation will rise up against nation, and kingdom against kingdom. There will be earthquakes in various places, and famines. These are the beginning of birth pains. But you, be on your guard! They will hand you over to Sanhedrin's, and you will be flogged in the synagogues. You will stand before governors and kings because of Me, as a witness to them. And the good news must first be proclaimed to all nations. So when they arrest you and hand you over, don't worry beforehand what you* *will say. On the contrary, whatever is given to you that hour say it. For it isn't you speaking, but the Holy Spirit. Then <u>brother will betray brother to death,</u> and a <u>father his child.</u> Children will <u>rise up against parents</u> and put them <u>to death.</u> And you will be <u>hated by everyone</u> because of My name. But the one who <u>endures</u> to the end will be <u>delivered.</u> When you see the abomination that causes desolation standing where it should not (let the reader understand), then those in Judea must <u>flee</u> to the mountains! A man on the housetop must not come down or go in to get anything out of his house. And a man in the field must not go back to get his clothes. <u>Woe to pregnant</u> women and <u>nursing</u> mothers in those days! Pray it won't happen in winter. For those will be <u>days of tribulation,</u> the kind that hasn't been from the beginning of the world, which God created, until now and never will be again! Unless the <u>Lord limited those days,</u> no one would survive. But He limited those days because of the elect, whom He chose. Then if anyone tells you, 'Look, here is the Messiah! Look there!' Do not believe it! For <u>false messiahs</u> and <u>false prophets will rise up</u> and will perform <u>signs</u> and <u>wonders</u> to <u>lead astray,</u> if possible, the elect. And <u>you must watch!</u> I have told you everything in advance. But in those days, after that tribulation: The <u>sun will be darkened,</u> and the <u>moon will not shed its light;</u> the <u>stars will be falling</u> from the sky, and the <u>celestial powers</u> will be <u>shaken.</u> Then they will see the Son of Man coming in clouds with great power and glory. He will send out the angels and gather His elect from the four winds, from the end of the earth to the end of the sky. Learn this parable from the fig tree: As soon as its branches becomes tender and sprouts leaves, you know that summer is near. In the same way, when you see these things happening, know that He is near at the door! I assure you: This <u>generation will</u> certainly <u>not pass</u> away until all these things take place. Heaven and earth will pass away, but My words will never pass away. Now concerning that day or hour no one knows neither the angels in heaven nor the Son-except the Father. <u>Watch! Be alert!</u> For you don't know when the time is coming.*

(Luke 21:8-36 NLT). *He replied, Don't let anyone mislead you, for many will come in my name, claiming, 'I am the Messiah,' and saying, 'The time has come!' But don't believe them. And when* you _hear of wars_ and insurrections, _don't panic._ Yes, these things must take place first, but the end won't follow immediately. Then he added, Nation will go to _war_ against nation, and kingdom against kingdom. There will be great _earthquakes,_ and there will be _famines_ and _plagues_ in many lands, and there will be _terrifying things_ and great _miraculous signs from heaven._ But before all this occurs, there will be a _time of great persecution._ You will be _dragged_ into synagogues and _prisons,_ and you will _stand trial_ before kings and governors because you are my followers. But this will be your opportunity to tell them about me. So don't worry in advance about how to answer the charges against you, for I will give you the _right words_ and such _wisdom_ that none of your opponents will be able to reply or refute you! Even those closest to you- your parents, brothers, relatives, and friends- _will betray you._ They will _even kill_ some of you. And _everyone will hate you_ because you are my followers. But not a hair of your head will perish! By _standing firm,_ you will win your souls. And when you see Jerusalem _surrounded by armies,_ then you will know that the _time of its destruction_ has arrived. Then those in Judea must _flee_ to the hills. Those in Jerusalem must get out, and those out in the country should not return to the city. For those will be _days of God's vengeance,_ and the prophetic words of the Scriptures will be fulfilled. How _terrible_ it will be for _pregnant_ women and for _nursing_ mothers in those days. For there will be _disaster in the land_ and _great anger_ against this people. They will be _killed by the sword_ or sent away as _captives_ to all the nations of the world. And Jerusalem will be _trampled_ down by the Gentiles until the period of the Gentiles comes to an end. And there will be _strange signs in the sun, moon and stars._ And here on earth the nations will be in _turmoil,_ perplexed by the roaring seas and _strange tides._ People will be _terrified_ at what they see coming upon the earth, for the _powers in the heavens will be shaken._ Then everyone will see the Son of Man coming on a cloud with power and great glory. So when all these things begin to happen, stand and look up, for your _salvation is near!_ Then he gave them this illustration: Notice the fig tree, or any other tree. When the leaves come out, you know without being told that summer is near. In the same way, when you see all these things taking place, you can know that the _Kingdom of God is near._ I tell you the truth, this _generation will not pass_ from the *scene until all these things have taken place. Heaven and earth will disappear, but my words will never disappear. <u>Watch out!</u> Don't let your hearts be dulled by carousing and drunkenness, and by the worries of this life. Don't let that day catch you unaware, like a trap. For that day will come upon everyone living on the earth. <u>Keep alert</u> at all times. And <u>pray</u> that you might <u>be strong</u> enough to escape these coming horrors and stand before the Son of Man.*

Jesus has mentioned "famine (poverty) and plagues or pesilence (pandemics & epidemics)". We have always struggled with plagues and famines on our planet. Let's look at these plagues within the last 500 years, from 1522 to 2022:

Cocoliztli epidemic (1545-1548),

Plague of London (1665-1666),

Plague of Marseille (1720-1723),

Russian plague (1770-1772),

Yellow Fever epidemic (1793)

First Cholera pandemic (1817-1824),

Second Cholera pandemic (1827-1835),

Third Cholera pandemic (1839-1856),

Fourth Cholera pandemic (1863-1875),

Fifth Cholera pandemic (1881-1886),

FLU pandemic (1889-1890),

Russian FLU (1889-1893),

Sixth Cholera pandemic (1899-1923),

POLIO epidemic (1916),

Spanish FLU (1918-1919),

Asian FLU (1957-1959),

Seventh Cholera pandemic (1961),

Honk Kong FLU (1968-1970),

AIDS pandemic (1981-present),

Severe Acute Respiratory Syndrome (SARS) (2002-2004),

Swine FLU, H1N1 (2009-2010)   EBOLA epidemic (2014-2016),

Middle East Respiratory Syndrome   Zika (2015-present)
(MERS) (2012-present),

Coronavirus (COVID-19) (2019-present)

This looks like a red flag warning sign to me. This is not even an exhaustive list and each one of these are responsible for tens of hundreds of thousands if not millions of deaths. Because of a past plague we take annual "flu shots" and childhood booster shots. I see the same thing with our recent COVID outbreak.

Most of what our Lord spoke about has been escalating since the beginning of the Church Age and Christianity, from the first century to the present. There have always been wars of conquest, great persecutions, and divisions within families, along with starvations and natural disasters. We have also seen strange signs in the sun, moon and stars. We cannot forget several false prophets (teachers/ pastors) as well as false messiahs from our past and present. They were going on in the first century as well as in our days. These events have been going on for over two thousand years. So when Jesus said, "This generation will (surely) not pass away," what was he talking about?

In Matthew and Mark they clearly wanted us to know that this particular generation will Not pass away. This was placed between the defilement of the Holy place and the fleeing from Judea. The only difference may be that all these things have been magnified and made worse throughout the years. So, the two things that still have not happened yet are; the (Gentile or non-Jewish unbelievers actual) desecration of the Holy Temple and the fleeing of the Jews from Judea. This is not to be confused with what went on during the first century. The Romans were known to display themselves as gods, even to the point of putting up statues of themselves in the Temple. This was not done in a human form or in the flesh. There was also the fleeing of the persecuted churches from everywhere, not just from Judea. This land mass was not fully populated yet with the Israelites. Though they were spread out through this geographical area, it is believe that this was a small picture of the things to come when the real antichrist shows

9

up. Both Israel and Palestinian have been battling to keep control of this Holy site, known as the Dome of the Rock, which is the main reason for the failed peace agreement. Neither side wants to give up this control. Even though the Palestinians already has their own three plus holy sites, they still want to claim more. Meanwhile Israel does not even have one, and the Dome of the Rock is rightfully theirs. From the first century to the 21st century, these two things have still not happened yet.

The use of the sword as a method of beheading execution has increased in popularity. I have seen the horrible aftermaths. A lot of scholars view this as symbolic of imminent death in general at the first century writings and for the readers understanding. But in light of the current events in the world more theologians believe that this should be taken literally.

Again all of these events spoken of by Christ will affect both unbelievers and believers. It is very important when studying these things to know who is saying what to whom and why. This needs to be seen as an overall big picture of the speaker and the listener(s) at the time frames and era. Why the statements are being said or why the question(s) were being asked.

What is a generation according to the Bible: 40, 100, and sometimes 70 years? As the sun was setting, Abram fell into a deep sleep, and a thick and dreadful darkness came over him. Then the Lord said to him, "Know for certain that for four hundred years your descendants will be strangers in a country not their own and that they will be enslaved and mistreated there… *In the fourth generation your descendants will come back here…* **(Genesis 15:16).**

God said to Abraham that after 400 years He would deliver Israel, "…in the fourth generation." A generation in the Bible is normally 40 years. However, here a generation is 100 years (4 × 100 = 400 years). This is understood by virtue of the fact that Abraham had his promised child when he was exactly 100 years old **(Genesis 21:5)**; it is evident, therefore, that the age of a man when his first child is born is the raw definition of a generation.

Nevertheless, notice that the full number (400 years) is exactly ten-times that of a regular generation of 40 years. Both 100 years and 40 years are a generation in the Bible. However, the average of these two is 70 years, which on occasion, is also found in the Bible, **(Psalm**

90:10). But "70 years" is a generation according to the average age of a man at his death, rather than when his first child is born (as with the example of Abraham).

40 + 100 = 140 years. 140 ÷ 2 = 70 years as a generation.

Two genealogical records are supplied of the generations that lived during the long stay in Egypt. The first lists four names and perhaps is a partial list. It was given immediately before the plagues of Egypt began (**Exodus 6:13-27,** and recurs in **1 Chronicles 6:1-3)**. This list covers Levi to Moses. The second has ten generations of names, **1 Chronicles 7:20-27.** This list covers Ephraim to Joshua's father, Nun. Joshua is the 11th name listed here because he represents the generation in the wilderness (40 years) since he leads the succeeding generation in Canaan land. Hence, we see that the four generation of names (4 × 100 = 400 years) represents the four generations in Egypt foretold by God. The 10 generation of names represent the same, but as 10 × 40 (400 years) with the following 40 years of desert wandering accounted to Joshua. The name "Joshua" is a variant of the name "Yeshua".

To summarize: A generation in the Bible is primarily the age of a man when his first male child is born; but secondarily, the age of a man at his death. The Bible then rounds the exact span of years in a "generation" to be 40 and 100 years as the primary usage, but on occasion, "70 years". And 70 is the average of 40 and 100, which allow the three timeframes to work in numeric harmony to produce the numeric symmetry found throughout the bible. The usage of the 100- year generation predominates in the Bible prior to the time of Moses when men lived longer, but 40 years used after Moses. A generation of 70 years is also referred to in the book of Enoch and of the Jubilees, and is highly compatible with the jubilee system of the Bible itself **(Daniel 9)**.

Though, some believe that a generation equals between 20 and as high as 30 years, it is simply not true. Some say that the Bolshevik Revolution in 1917 was the seed (birth pains) that was planted and how Israel got its start to become a nation in 1948. If this is the case the 100 year generation would have expire in 2017. Or this generational period could have also started when Israel actually became a nation in

1948, expiring in 2048. It is also well to note that there were a lot of immigrants and minorities in Russia that were of Jewish descendant, as well as in other surrounding European countries.

If we were to look at a map of where Judea is located you would see that it is bordered right in Palatine controlled territory (Syria), on Israel's side. There are presently close to 500,000 thousand Jews living in this occupied land area known as Judea. The two States mutually agreed to allow for a time frame not to uproot these Jewish families living in Judea.

From 1948, when Israel finally became a nation and in June of 1967, their borders were largely expanded, during the Six Day War. This would be an example of what God told the **Israelites in Joshua 1:11,** to go in and take possession (or control) of the land. Israel had the opportunity to take what God gave them, but they fail to take the Dome of the Rock when they had the chance and later ended up giving it back and lost most of the land in the years ahead. I believe that this will soon come to an end when the agreement is recanted. This may have a lot to do with the soon to be peace agreement, of seven years; or at least it plays a big part of it. Then there will be an all out war in the region, during the mid-point (3 1/2 years). When we see these two things happen, this generation will be cut down to just under a seven year life span. So both of these two things are the only things missing and must/will go together, in the very near future; for this generation.

> **Zechariah 12:2-4,** prophecy refers to what is going on in our mists. *"I am going to make Jerusalem a cup that sends all the surrounding peoples reeling. Judah will be besieged as well as Jerusalem. On that day when all the nations of the earth are gathered against her, **I will** make Jerusalem an immovable rock for all the nations. All who try to move it will injure themselves. On that day **I will** strike every horse with panic and its rider with madness, declares the Lord. **I will** keep a watchful eye over the house of Judah, but **I will** blind all the horses of the nations."*

The land that was given to Israel in 1948 was a minute sliver from the original promise of God. According to the Old Testament the "Promise Land" went from the Nile River in Egypt and eastward towards the Euphrates River; covering a quarter of the northern part of Saudi Arabia (some say it covered half of this country). It continued upward north taking half of Iraq (some believe it covered all of Iraq), going east taking about 60 percent of Syria (or all of Syria), all of Jordan and parts of southern Turkey and stopping at the Mediterranean Sea. Israel literally tripled in size from 1948 and after the six day war in 1967. They were gaining what God originally promised His people (about a 3rd), but they failed to seek God like king David did; instead, they heeded to human counsel the following decade in the short Yom Kippur war (1973). The Nixon Administration told Israel not to shoot first, unless shot upon. In the end they lost 2,200 men with 3,000 wounded. They also lost some of the land they had gained earlier. In the 1980's they lost even more land to become the size of what they are today.

We cannot possibly count all the false prophets and messiahs that rose and fell from the past to the present. Apostle John was the first to coin the term or phrase antichrist.

1 John 2:18

you have heard that <u>antichrist</u> shall come, even now there are many <u>antichrists</u>.

1 John 2:22;

He is the <u>antichrist</u>, that denies the Father and the Son,

1 John 4:3

every spirit that confesses not that Jesus Christ is come in the flesh is not of God: and this is that <u>spirit of antichrist,</u> whereof you have heard that it should come; and is already in the world. Again he writes in

2 John 7,

<u>many deceivers</u> are entered into the world, who confess not that Jesus Christ is come in the flesh. This is a <u>deceiver</u> and an <u>antichrist</u>.

Paul refers to antichrist as the man of lawlessness and the son of perdition (**2 Thessalonians chapter 2**). Antichrist may mean either an enemy of Christ or one who usurps Christ's name and rights. He will be that which completely refuses and denies Christ regardless of the evidence. They will fight, attack and rebel by any means possible, even to kill with violence. Or to turn against one's own family by reporting believers to authorities (Hitler did that during World War II, dividing children against parents). This has nothing to do with the lost and the unchurched that we are to still witness. It is our job to be missionaries regardless of the cost.

There is some confusion about what John and Paul were talking about. This is not referring to an actual antichrist as per a person. They are referring to the "spirit" of antichrist, in the same way as the spirit of Balaam (compromise) and the spirit of Koran (rebellion); likewise the spirit of Jezebel (control). This antichrist will eventually manifest himself into a condensed bodily form at the appointed time.

One belief says that there was or will be a total of three actual main antichrists in bodily form after everything is completed. The Bible does not substantiate this theory. The first was believed to be Napoleon, the second one was Hitler, the next up and coming third and final one is going to be much worst. Each one of them has or will fool a lot of people. Jesus warned us in John's Gospel:

> *If you find the godless world is hating you, remember it got its start hating Me. If you lived on the world's terms, the world would love you as one of its own. But since I picked you to live on God's terms and no longer on the world's term, the world is going to hate you. When that happens, remember this: Servants don't get better treatment then their masters. If they beat on Me, they will certainly beat on you. If they did what I told them, they will do what you tell them* (**John 15:20 MSG**).

Evil is evil, it will always try to influence the world.

> Jesus foretells of His second coming; *they will say to you, 'Look there! Look here!' Do not go away, and do not run after them. For just like the lightning, when it flashes out of the sky, shines to the other part of the sky, so will the Son of Man be in His day. But first He must suffer many things and be rejected by this generation. And just as it happened in the days of Noah, so it will be also in the days of the Son of Man: they were eating, they were drinking, they were marrying, they were being given in marriage, until the day that Noah entered the ark and the flood came and destroyed them all. It was the same as in the days of Lot: they were eating, they were drinking, they were buying, they were selling, they were planting, they were building; but on the day that Lot went out from Sodom it rained fire and brimstone from heaven and destroyed them all. It will be just the same on the day that the Son of Man is revealed. On that day, the one who is on the housetop and whose goods are in the house must not go down to take them out; and likewise the one who is in the field must not turn back, (Remember Lot's wife). Whoever seeks to keep his life will lose it, and whoever loses his life will preserve it. I tell you, on that night there will be two in one bed; one will be taken and the other will be left. There will be two*

women grinding at the same place; one will be taken and the other will be left. Two men will be in the field; one will be taken and the other will be left (**Luke 17:23-36 NASB**).

Just from 1900 to about 2015, various people have claimed to, in fact be the Messiah. The Synoptic gospels (**Matthew 24:4, 6, 24; Mark 13:5, 21-22;** and **Luke 21:3**) all use the term *pseudochristos* for messianic pretenders. This list would excludes many of the past and present false prophets and false teachers (clergy's) which are beyond many. This is not an exhaustive list.

Lou de Palingboer (Louwrens Voorthuijzen) (1898–1968)

Father Divine (George Baker) (1880–1965)

André Matsoua (1899–1942)

Samael Aun Weor (1917–1977)

Ahn Sahng-hong (1918–1985)

Sun Myung Moon (1920–2012)

Cho Hee-Seung (1931–2004)

Yahweh ben Yahweh (Hulon Mitchell Jr.) (1935-2007)

Laszlo Toth (1938-2012)

Wayne Bent (Michael Travesser) (born 1941)

Iesu Matayoshi (1944–2018)

Jung Myung Seok (born 1945)

José Luis de Jesús (1946–2013)

Inri Cristo (Alvaro Thais) (born 1948)

Apollo Quiboloy (born 1950)

Brian David Mitchell, (born 1953)

Ante Pavlovic (1959-2020)

David Koresh (Vernon Wayne Howell) (1959–1993)

Sergey Torop (born 1961)

Maria Devi Christos (born 1960)

Allen John Miller (born 1963)

Since the beginning of sin entering the world, there has always been violence with His creation. It does not seem like it has ever stopped or changed, only in our perfecting and affecting our own abilities to kill and destroy each other better. History keeps on repeating this over and over, and it's been getting increasingly worst. Think about this, every technology that has ever been created or invented started off for mankind's good. When technologies tend to stick around long enough, they start becoming evil in the minds and hands of humans. Another point I would like to make is that our founding fathers were totally brilliant intellectuals, well beyond their own years and time. They all came together in one thought, mind, and purpose in order to create a once Great Nation. Their writings and what they fought for and believed in are now being torn and destroyed more in this present generation. If God would not have held back the knowledge of technology in their days, we would not be alive today, because they would have destroyed one another and this planet.

Think of the Wright brothers. In 1903 they invented the airplane flight and aerodynamics was born. In a matter of about ten years we used this same invention that was for good and turned it into something evil, by shooting bullets and dropping bombs to kill people during World War I (1914-1918).

As long as evil exists in our world, our hands are forced to try to prevent the spread of this sickness. It is our moral obligation to stand to fight against all manner of evil, not to lie down and do nothing. Whether we like it or not we are facing wars and battles every day, either within us or all around us. God forbid we just sit in our comfy little pews and close our eyes, thinking and hoping it might all go away. Yet that is what this generational church has done as a whole... nothing. Even with all the electronic devices that started off as a good thing, it is now frying and destroying our generation's mind. Overindulgence is not a good thing. Thank God that there still remains remnants of God's true people that did something. God is a God of warfare and battles; check the Old Testament. We should have the whole armor of God on and be battle ready **(Ephesians 6:10-18)**. Along with technology, human dysfunction seems to follow. Yes, our marriages and families are being destroyed. Divorces are out of control, marriages are becoming old fashion and obsolete. There is a fear of commitments or fear of failure, verses just shacking up. We are warriors of the right and proper kind, meaning there is and will be a time to use spiritual weapons, lots of prayers and actions with pure motives. We have never really learned to just get along or work together across these denominational lines. There is Not a pure and perfect denomination, so get over yourself. We all have fallen short. Remember the foundation is Jesus Christ and the Word of God... PERIOD. It is the things that are built on that foundation that are worrisome, a lot of human rules and regulations.

God's hand of mercy has actively limited and stopped evil from fully spreading throughout the earth. The Bible refers to a "Cup of God's Wrath"; depending on the translation it is also called "Anguish, Agonize, Dread or Iniquity" (**Jeremiah 25:15-17; Psalms 75:8; Habakkuk 2:16; Zechariah 12:2-3;** and **Revelation 16:19, 18:6**) Some scholars believe that this was the same type of cup that Jesus had to drink from in **Matthew 26:38-39; Luke 22:41-46;** and **John 18:11**. The full measure of the cost for our sin had to be paid for in full. Greed and sexual immorality has been planted deeply when man fell hard away from God. The days of Noah and Lot are clearly upon us today, without any cares in the world. Nowhere did Jesus say we would Not suffer or go through these trials, tribulations, sufferings, and persecutions. On the contrary He said that we would go through issues and problems in life. They persecuted Christ and they will persecute you! It is unavoidable (unfortunately), it is life. The other thing to mention is that Jesus was talking to "only" His disciples during these special meetings. So the Endtimes "will" affect both believers and unbelievers.

So why should believers be so concerned about the "Endtimes", if it has nothing to do with them? After all a lot of them say, hey we will be "Raptured out of here." Many Christians say, hey I'm good I got my ticket to Heaven. You're on your own, figure it out, oh and good luck. We are only given the opportunity to know and understand the Signs of the Times beforehand. I am talking about prior to God's "Wrath." The main ideas are to be sober and watchful. These things will and are happening, so don't be shocked or amazed as they come upon you. There will be personal attacks because of your Christianity; but also because of the coldness and hardness of their hearts, they will attack each other. Selfishness and greed will be wide spread like a cancer. Folks we thought were our friend will turn against us. This would include our neighbors, coworkers and close relatives (siblings and even our own parents). We won't be able to trust anyone, but God. We have gotten to the point that we have been and are now murdering (sacrificing) our own children on the altar of Molech (an Old Testament pagan god) through abortions and other forms of abuses. The evening news has reported parents drowning, suffocating, molesting, beating and selling their own children.

Our children are no longer the blessings that God intended for us. On the contrary our minds became greedier and can only see dollar signs of what we can get out of our children, such as child support or government assisted programs. We need to cleave to God, He will never leave or forsake His children. We should not be fearful or have a sense of loneliness. You have the Holy Spirit in you, poured out according to the scriptures (**Isaiah 32:15-16, Ezekiel 36:25-27, Hosea 3:5, Joel 2:28, Micah 4:1, Acts 2:28, Titus 3:4-6,** and **2 Peter 3:3**). You will be able to stand firm in all the truth with peace, power and boldness. So we should look forward to (not to run away from) these things as an opportunity to advance the kingdom of God. So what He spoke of can easily be paralleled with the Seals and Trumpets, such as; wars, famine, earthquakes, family betrayal, and shortening of the days (sun and moon) among others. It is not just earthquakes that Jesus warned us about. It is natural disasters that are increasing at an alarming rate. It is a wakeup call for the churches to get busy in Kingdom business.

Whatever comes, know that God is in control, He will protect and provide for our needs. During these events we are still not helpless or defenseless.

> Jesus said in **John 14:27** *"Peace I leave with you, My peace I give to you. I do not give it to you as the world does. Do not let your heart be troubled (distressed) or lacking in courage".*

Those that have been martyred in the past had this same kind of peace, in order to do the things they did. I believe that this will be God's way of preparing His bride for the wedding. He will transform us as spotless brides through our trials (**2 Corinthians 4:8-9**).

Let's face it, we are not even close to being spotless. A true bride dresses in pure white not off white or egg shell white. This will cause a great falling away as God purges and sifts the impurities within each and every Christian (**2 Thessalonians 2:3),** if we so allow Him to.

It is so sad that a lot of Christians would rather keep and enjoy their sinful nature, all the while God is saying No, all you need is Me; I demand Holiness (to be separate, different). Through this process, it will separate the real and the fake children of God within our mists. There will be no more riding the fence or gray areas for church goers, it is all in, sold out for Jesus Christ or nothing. I see some of that going on today with a lot of the church members, when they don't get their own way or are confronted by an issue. They would either move on to another church or cause divisions, rather than fix and improve themselves. Let alone change for the better. Nonbelievers do see this and it is a complete turn off. They do not want anything to do with this so called god of theirs. At this point in time there are too many secret sins dwelling within our mists. Our hearts and attitudes among the saved and the lost are suffering and God is dealing with this.

Since God is a God of unity and harmony, even the best church is not without some kind of discourse. In the Old Testament it took Esther twelve months preparation for her wedding day (**Esther 2:12**). God can and could very well be doing the same thing for His church bride, getting us ready for the Rapture. I truly feel that even though the Rapture is very close, it cannot or will not happen until the church is ready.

If the Rapture were to happen today a large percentage of us would miss it. The Rapture is completely different from just being saved and going to Heaven. So it is never about the Heaven or Hell issue. If you and I being saved were to die we will go to Heaven, or if unsaved Hell. It is simply viewing this around the Feast, Wedding, and Bride aspect.

There has also been a lot of confusion surrounding the Wrath of God which is truly a no brainer. The believers and followers of Christ are not (never were) subject to God's Wrath. There is nowhere in scripture where God has ever poured out His Wrath on any righteous man or mankind. It is totally profound to think of God as evil or mean, after all that His Son went through and did for us, and then just throw it all away. There are no bases or foundation to even conceive any such thing to conclude that God would even consider such a motive. I personally have not come across any proof or evidence to say otherwise.

Some examples of God's Wrath, happened during Noah's day during the Great Flood in **Genesis 6.** He removed or protected the righteous before His Wrath; and also during Abraham's day to rescue Lot, God intervened, when God's Wrath destroyed Sodom and Gomorrah in **Genesis 19**. Do you see a pattern? It all had to do with evil people. Only then the Cup of God's Wrath was over flowing. Even after Jonah's warning upon Nineveh, it only lasted for about 150 years, before God's Wrath did destroy it (see **Nahum**).

The days of Job's testing, between God and Satan was not His Wrath. Of the many attributes of God, holy, mercy, grace, and justice are more prevailing and abundant; evil is not a part of God's purpose or planning. He has always been quick to forgive and His mercy is forever, at the same time He is slow to anger. He will warn, correct, and/or chastise us; we can see this throughout the Bible. God's Wrath is solely reserved for Satan, his angels and every ungodliness and unrighteousness under Heaven. So if you belong to any one of these groups, you might want to reconsider your position while you have time and before it is too late. There is no benefit or pleasure for God to destroy any of us to hell, which is what His Wrath is all about. He desires true repentance. On the other hand, there is mankind's wrath and Satan's wrath; and God limits their destruction. Those are for God's glory as witnesses and a testimony upon all the earth. God is love and Satan is evil; this will not and has never changed.

The other issue surrounds the last trumpet call. First the Scriptures states that it was an actual trumpet sound, not like a voice or something that is likened to mimic this musical instrument. The second thing is that there is a last sound of the trumpet, meaning there has to be at least more than one sounding. The Bible does not clearly tell us the number of Trumpets other than in the book of Revelation; only that there is more than one. I as well as most theologians do believe this to be a total of "Seven" trumpet sounds. This belief refers to the fact that the number "7" is God's number for total absolute completion. And it would have to be in harmony and unity with God's character. You can see: **I Corinthians 15:51-52** and **I Thessalonians 4:15-17**. Also in **Matthew 24:31**, Jesus Himself says "...with a great sound of A trumpet,..." It says an actual trumpet!

I don't believe we will be capable to actually hear these Trumpets, at least not with physical ears, since God is Spirit, it must be with Spiritual ears (hearing). God is a purposeful God. The Bible does not say that we would be able to hear any other trumpets, but alludes only to the last trumpet.

All we have to go on are the actual signs and the described evident that they were sounded. The only one we might hear would and can be the seventh (or last) Trumpet. Those that are alive and those that are dead believers will hear this Trumpet. One of the events most taken out of context in scriptures involves God's Wrath and the Trumpet. I cannot twist it to benefit me; it would be a lie. Many people are hung up on **Revelation 4:1,** when God called John up to Himself, with or like a "voice" like a trumpet, so He can show him things to come. God's voice is also thunderous and roars like rushing waters **(Job 40:9** & **Revelation 14:2).** God has several tunes/voices just like we have, it is all part of our God given DNA; from our moods, emotions, feelings, and level of position (authority). God also has a soft still/gentle **(I King 19:11-13)** (Daddy) voice too. The one thing I could not wrap my thoughts around, was the impact regarding the pregnant and nursing mothers **(Matthew 24:19, Mark 13:17** & **Luke 21:23).** Any time God mentions something in His Word, it is always important; if it's three times, it is extremely important.

ISIS is the most barbaric, ruthless terrorist group on the face of the planet. It has been reported that they kill every man, woman and child that does not believe or conform to the ways of Allah. It was reported that any pregnant women they come across, they have cut opened their bellies, removing the unborn child and hang them by their umbilical cords onto trees as a horrific message. It is unimaginable what will happen to the pregnant women and the tiny babies in the days ahead.

The words "Fear Not" I have been told is mentioned 365 times in the Bible. That would equal one for each day of the year. Though I only came up with 333, that is still a lot. Yes, there will be a lot of junk happening in the world, like the days of Noah and Lot. Selflessness and common sense will be a thing in the past; it is going to get crazier. Not to worry, keep your focus on God; you are not hopeless or defenseless. That is the main purpose of His Gifts and His Holy Spirit inside of you. God did not and *does not give us the spirit of fear; but of Love, Power and of a Sound Mind* (**2 Timothy 1:7**).

Of all of our valuables and possessions, the most critical in our hands must be our Bibles. The only thing that needs to matter will be the Word of God and not stuff. There are approximately 7.182 billion people on planet earth, as of 2013. Of that, it is estimated that only about 2.1 billion claim to be Christians. That in itself can be debatable, depending on one's definition. You are either a follower of Jesus Christ or you're not, anything else would be a lie or false. God keeps it simple, while humans make it confusing or difficult. When the time to Rapture the Church comes, not all of them will be Raptured. It is easy to say you are something, when you might not be. There are only two sure easy ways to tell a fake Christian from the real ones. **John 13:35**: *they will know that you are My disciple by your love for one another, and you would know them by their fruits* (**Galatians 5:22-23**). It is not the original intent to just love other believers, what good would that be? Or about singing and listening to Christian music, reading and studying the Bible, watching Christian entertainment, or fellowshipping with other Christians. Though these are things that every Christian should be doing, plus a whole lot more. This love is the same kind of love Jesus displayed, compassion for the lost. We are to love everyone not just the select few in our little clicks. Jesus loved the unlovable. As for the fruits, we will be responsible for and will answer to them at the Judgment. We are to equip the called and to advance the Kingdom of God. Wearing religious clothing, jewelry, and sporting a tattoo does not make you a Christian; that is all outward stuff. It is what is on the inside that matters. Remember even atheists can be nice people. And demons believe and are still going to hell. We are in the world, but not of it. There must be first and foremost a firm solid foundation. God has made it so simple and basic for everyone.

Confessing with our mouth and believing in our heart, that Jesus saved you from death to life (**Romans 10:9**); and to be Lord over everything in your life. The confessing part is an action verb requiring works,; they're not just idol words. This has everything to do with an inward relationship between Creator and creation that overflows outwardly to love others and an outward works of the Fruits of the Spirit. Going from slave or servant of sin, to a slave or servant for Jesus Christ; to understand the full magnitude of this transition you should study what He went through the last twenty-four to forty-eight hours on planet earth. It was the penalties for our sins He never committed; the crucial and agonizingly painful beatings, up to and including His death upon the Roman cross. The great news is that He rose to victory for us. Even though we may see, hear or go through these things, being Saved makes all the difference. We were never promised an easy life. Each and every Christian needs to make their relationship personal.

The Church has justified some empty formulated words to create the "Sinner's Prayer." The churches may have meant well but only God truly knows the heart of the individuals. It is just unscriptural and has been totally taken out of content. The road paved with good intentions still leads to Hell. Yes, we are to confess and repent (turn from) of our sins first to God and then to each other.

It is believed that it was the Protestant denominations in the 1850's that came up with the whole sinner's prayer theory in their bylaws. It wasn't until around the 1920's that the other massive denominations followed suit. This has become one of the biggest and most dangerous lies inside the churches. I say this with the utmost respect because this is a very sensitive area. Prior to the 1850's I have not been able to find any evidence in supporting the sinner's prayer. I even reviewed the First (1730's-1770's) and Second (1790's-1840's) Great Awakenings. There must be a change that follows confessing and repentance. Thinking you are okay and all is good just because you repeated some words is so wrong and very dangerous. What good is it if you are still sinning? I have met countless people claiming to be a Christian, but the proof says otherwise. Without change, their faith is dead.

Do not believe everything that comes across your ears and tries to take root in your heart. Guard your hearts (**Proverbs 4:23**) and work out your own Salvation (**Philippians 2:12**). This is an individual responsibility.

One church believes that they are the only denomination that will get to Heaven, while all the others are doomed to hell. Another refers to the Holy Spirit as an "It" not a He. Another thing that is going around is, in order to get to Heaven the individual has to speak in tongues and also be baptized; a prerequisite for entering the kingdom of God. All you have to do to believe in your heart and confess (works a.k.a doing) with your mouth, then you're good to go. Another belief denies major parts of the medical professions. They say surgeries and blood transfusions are off limits, yet it is okay to seek the minor things such as eye doctors or dentists for assistance. In my opinion you can't have both, it just doesn't make sense. One denomination will preach separately from the Bible. While still others believe it is okay to pray to different saints or to the Virgin Mary. Also some claim that there are many different gods; god of nature, god of fertility, sun or moon gods etc. Or that the King James Version is the only true translation. Some religions even play with out of body experiences or putting curses on others. The list goes on and on, there is no single perfect religion. There are over 34,000 known Christ like denominations on this planet as of 2015, and every one of them are flawed. No disrespect, but my Bible says I (we) can boldly go before the Throne room of God **(Hebrews 4:16)**. Jesus is all we need, the Holy Spirit is our guide and God is our Father; what else can we possibly need that is left undone? Jesus said, that; "It is Finished" **(John 19:30)** He meant what He said. There is nothing else left to do but believe, all is completed. Doctrines come and go but God's words are everlasting.

The Bible commonly refers to Christians (followers of Christ) as sheep. How are sheep different from all the other animals? The description is as follows; they need plenty of water, they must be lead to food. Dirt remains on them until someone or something else cleans them. They must be sheared for their own good, if they fall they cannot get up on their own; they would need outside assistance. They are easily restless and are defenseless or helpless having no sharp teeth or fangs, no claws or horns; only soft fluffy wool. They are weak and directionless (will get lost easily), they are not intelligent. They only follow (know) the shepherd's voice and sheep are also a precious possession.

The point I am making is compared to God we are dumb and weak. It doesn't matter how smart you think you are: you are not. We require plenty of Living Water, we should be lead to eat the Word of God as our only Spiritual food. We stunk in sin until Jesus cleansed us with His Blood. We are constantly being pruned through the renewing of our mind's as well as our Spiritual growth for our own good (trials). When we fall only the Holy Spirit and or other believers can help us up again. Without the Peace of God in our lives, we become restless and fearful. We are defenseless against the enemy without Spiritual weapons (**Ephesians 6:10-18**). We are weak but are made strong in Christ. We were once directionless but now we have a purpose and a divine destiny as God shines His light guiding our path. If any of us lack Wisdom all we have to do is ask Him that gives abundantly. We should be following Christ's (voice) leading us as our only Shepherd; the high price to save us, we became His very own possession. We may still be considered His sheep, but we are far from the hopeless state that we came from.

Like all of the books in the Bible, Genesis alone covers in the neighborhood of about 1500 years. The four Gospel books covers around 33 years, the life of Christ. A lot of commentators believe that the book of Acts is still very much active and continuing today. Likewise, the book of Revelation has its own timeline that it covers 2000 years plus. It seems to be more spread out up until we have gotten to this point. Things are now happening faster as we get closer to the End.

Also, keep in mind that the number "Seven" is God's perfect number for perfect completion and deliverance. God created all things in six days and rested on the seventh day. During the days of Jericho, God had Israel march once per day for six days; on the seventh day they marched around seven times. They also had seven priests blowing seven trumpet horns on that final march (**Joshua 6:1-4**). The number SEVEN is very important for our understanding.

Mankind is nearing the end of its soon to be six thousandth years on planet earth, after that will be the thousand years of rest. There is a reason or purpose as to why or how God is or does what He does. God has never ever carelessly just done anything.

Jesus has fulfilled the first four of the seven Hebrew feasts; the Passover, the Unleavened Bread, the First Fruits, and the Feast of Weeks or Pentecost (**Leviticus 23**). These were all accomplished from His crucifixion to His ascension, during the Spring time (March/April). This leaves the last three feasts; the Feast of Trumpets (the Last Trumpet will be sounding soon), the Day of Atonement (the

Wedding feast and the 1000 year Reign), and the Feast of Tabernacles (Eternality, paradise). Jesus will return to fulfill these. Most believe this will happen during the Fall season (September/October).

CHAPTER TWO

THE SEVEN SEALS; THE BEGINNING

THE SEVEN SEALS: a longer time period ending at Armageddon. The best way to understand Seals is to think of a document that carries a seal, such as a birth or death certificate, drivers or marriage license or educational degree. Or a contract agreement like purchasing a car or home, until the obligations are completed. The seals tell a longer timeline story. I have concluded that the Seals along with the Trumpets and the Vials refer to different lengths of time from one another, and that they will all end at Armageddon. They are found in three Revelation scriptures.

> **Revelation 8:5:** *Then the Angel took the censer, filled it with fire from the altar, and threw it to the earth. And there were* ***noises, thunderings, lightnings, and the earthquake.***

> **Revelation 11:19:** *Then the temple of God was opened in Heaven, and the Ark of the Covenant was seen in His temple. And there were* ***lightnings, noises, thunderings, and great hail.***

> And **Revelation 16:18:** *And there were* ***noises and thunderings and lightnings; and there was a great earthquake,*** *such a*

mighty and great earthquake as had not occurred since men were on the earth.

These verses are at the end of each of the three completed Sevens. They will start at different points in time and will end at Armageddon.

It is also very important to realize that John was not on Earth during these visions. He moved around, but mainly he was in Heaven looking down towards planet Earth. It was an actual bird's eye view from the lense of a first century man to a future generation. We need to put ourselves in his shoes and not the other way around. The Seals can be classified as the signs (warnings) of the Times, as foretold in prophecy.

It is also all about the delivery! Many times in the Bible, God's Wrath was a pouring out of something not a breaking of something or a blowing of something. Also, whenever God was to send or bring about His Wrath, it was always delivered through His Messengers. Angels were always sent to fulfill God's final Wrath. It was also Jesus that was the only one allowed to break and open these Seven Seals. Jesus is *Not* God's Angel! He is God's Son of the Trinity, King, Lord and High Priest. At the same time, Jesus was never sent to deliver these Seals as a Wrath as He never left Heaven.

God also uses what is known as a numbering system all through-out the Bible. The number "three" represents a complete wholeness, as in God is a three part Being: Father, Son, and Holy Spirit equal-ing One. Even Lucifer as: Satan, antichrist, and unholy spirit (false prophet). We are also three parts as well: body, soul, and spirit equal-ing one. The Seals, the Trumpets, and the Vials also equal one. We can also break this down even further: His warning signs (Seals), His judgment signs (Trumpets), and His Wrath (Vials) which equals one or complete wholeness. I would refer to the Seals as a wakeup (observ-able) call. The Trumpets would be a last chance as a time of humility and repentance. And the Vials represent your fate having been sealed.

One can see the parallels between **Revelation chapter 6** and through to parts of **chapter 15** and of the same things as in **Matthew chapter 24**. Both of them refer to wars, invasions, famines, earthquakes, and persecutions of Christians as **signs** that the End of the Age is approaching; the sun, moon, and stars will also be affected. Also see **Mark chapter 13**, **Luke chapter 21** and the second half of **Matthew chapter 10** (can also easily apply, some scholars overlook this passage). Signs of the times, are as God's warnings to us; and not necessarily God's Wrath on humanity. In Jesus' foretold prophecy, He never described or alluded that the vials or bowls would be something that Christians would go through. In fact Jesus stopped short of it and didn't even touch on the subject with His disciples, because we will be Raptured before they are *poured out* upon the earth. His description solely refers to the Seals and the Trumpets upon the earth.

Something else worth noting is that God is not subject to time; neither are His angels, demons or Satan. Remember that one day is like a thousand years and a thousand years are like a day to God (**2 Peter 3:8** and **Psalms 90:4**). He created time for us. His realm is outside of time. Everything is not going to happen within a close time period such as a few days, months or (Seven) years. Some of these signs and warnings will take centuries. It will happen slowly and gradually and are not totally known or seen until they happen.

Be Aware Of The New Normal! It has been getting crazier as common sense goes out the window. Is it really okay to murder unborn children? What about Critical Race Theory? Child sex trafficking? Attacking and murdering people all because they think differently? Is it okay to rob and destroy businesses? Now law and order has become the enemy? What about the lack of morality, as we keep pushing God further and further out of our society? He (God) is not allowed in our government or in our schools. During the last pandemic churches were forced to close due to them being deemed as non-essential, yet some bars, spas, and resturants (some businesses in general were allowed to stay open with their large crowds because they are somehow deemed essential?

Cancel culture today is not something new. They tried canceling Jesus Christ over 2000 years ago, because the religious elites did not want to hear it either. The churches were also being attacked in the first century. Canceling Doctor Seuss too, really? Why? Even social media sites like Facebook and their "fact checkers", that are attacking and oppressing our freedom of speech because it does not fit their narrative.

They canceled then president Trump from their site, as well as others. Actors like Scott Baio and Kevin Sorbo are trying to fight this injustice. Even I have spent time on Facebook probation and jail. I eventually just canceled them and moved on, I've got better things to do with my time. Our priorities are screwed up. We still have unalienable rights in our Constitution that God gave us in the Bible, not man. We have been surrendering without a fight, giving in to unlawful laws. As the end draws nearer they will speed up.

God is still merciful and still does not want any to perish. While most churches want to believe that all of these things are to take place within the Seven year Tribulation period; I have found no actual proof in the Bible to support this. First we must understand that the Book of Revelation is not solely based on a seven year time line (only **Daniel 9**, refers to these weeks). We first need to look at the overall big picture, since there are so many activities going on. God is still a God of order and of one accord, harmony and unity. So allow all the dust to settle in order to see what God desires to reveal to us.

"Above all else, guard (with all diligence-watch over) your heart, for it is the wellspring (issues-good and noble things) of life" **Proverbs 4:23.**

Revelation 1:1-2 *The Revelation of Jesus Christ, which God gave to Him to show to His servants things which must soon take place. He sent and signified it by His angel to His servant John, who bears record of the word of God, and of the testimony of Jesus Christ, and of all things that he saw.*

The book of Revelation is not just about foretelling events of the Endtimes. This book starts off as a Revelation or of a revealing of Jesus Christ. I believe one can see Him throughout the book of Revelation, but only if you are looking. God allows Jesus to show His servants, (that would be all believers) that we are to bear the truth of the word of God and to testify of Jesus Christ. In other words we are to "Be" His witnesses not to "Do" witnessing.

Revelation 1:3 *Blessed is the one who reads the words of this prophecy, and blessed are those who hear it and take to heart what is written in it, because the Time is Near.*

We are capable and able to hear and take to heart God's message of these perilous times. If it were not true, John would not have made this statement. So take heed and be blessed! Also, some believe that the events took place or happened shortly after John's writing. He described them as in the present realities regardless of when they may have occurred. Something we need to understand at the very beginning. In the Old Testament in relation to End Time prophecies, they have always referred to it as "The Latter Days" or in the far distance. Now at the start, John writes "The Time is Near" or closer. Jesus wants us to understand God is not a mystery towards us nor does He keep Himself from us (**Deuteronomy 29:29, Romans 16:25, I Corinthians 2:7-8, Ephesians 3:3-4, Colossians 4:3**). The mysteries and hidden secrets are kept from Satan, not from God's children. God is truly an open book towards His children that pursue and go after Him. If anyone lacks wisdom let them ask God, who will give generously to those who asks (**James 1:5**). Or if you hunger and thirst for righteousness (**Matthew 5:6**). Ask, seek, and knock (**Matthew 7:7**), all thing are possible, you just have to be willing to go after it.

Between Revelation chapters two and three, John writes to seven actual churches in his day. Some believe this is also in regards to the church age. Not just during the days of John but also into the future up to and including the Raptured event. Remember the number Seven is symbolic as it represents to spiritual perfection and completion. These seven churches were dealing with seven different kinds of spiritual attacks from the enemy; much like the attacks the churches are undergoing today, they were dealing with different types of spirits:

Ephesus was dealing with the spirit of religion   (2:4-7),

Smyrna was dealing with the spirit of intimidation   (2:10-11),

Pergamum was dealing with the <u>spirit of compromise</u>   (2:12-17),

Thyatira was dealing with the <u>spirit of (control) Jezebel</u>   (2:18-20, 26),

Sardis was dealing with the <u>spirit of traditionalism</u>   (3:1-6),

Philadelphia was dealing with the <u>spirit of inferiority</u>   (3:7-8, 12),

Laodicea was dealing with the <u>spirit of pride</u>   (3:14-17, 21).

These same spirits are still active in a lot of our churches today. There are two sure fired ways to know that they are not within your church. Number one is growth; an active advancement of God's Kingdom, not personal gain or ulterior motives. This is where God has freedom to move as He sees fit without set guidelines of programs, ceremonies, or rituals. Increase is definitely a factor in God's overall plan. Secondly, unity and harmony is a must within the body of believers with one focus in mind; the lost and the witness of the Gospel of Jesus Christ,— Kingdom business. We are not perfect in our ways and do make errors from time to time, know that the truth always wins. Genuine Godly love goes a long way when shown purely in all truths and obedience through ordained authority; no hypocritical attitudes. Even though these spirits do show up from time to time when confronted they must leave, in Jesus' name. This proves, they will not and have not quit in their attacks.

There are many warnings throughout the Bible about false prophets and teachers (**II Peter 2:1-2; Jude 4-19**). Just because one has a cross on a building, or claims Jesus Christ as their foundation, or even says that they are a Christian does not make it true. Personally, I cannot stand being called a Christian by name or in title, label, or position only. Christian was a name that the secular Roman government gave them. The believers simply referred to themselves as "The Way" or the Followers of Christ. So being a Christian in itself has been tainted. I am not just talking about the secular churches or some man made religion. I have visited several denominational churches, not all of them were bad but not all of them were good either. This has caused the true churches to become stigmatized from society. There is such a thing called "spiritual abuse," (Mars Hill Church in CO).

The last thing to understand is that the word gospel means more than "Good News." We have watered it down and by doing so, have made it meaningless. The original Greek definition is over the top, amazingly shocking in awe, too good to be true good news. I like to use the "far beyond measurable, impossible undeserving" Good News. So it would be far beyond getting a raise, landing a job, getting married, having a baby or completing a dream. This News is for everyone; we cannot earn it nor do we deserve it. This gift is of Salvation, of Hope, of Love, of Grace and of Mercy; to anyone who simply believes and receives. Christ is all inclusive to whosoever believes, not exclusive due to gender, nationality, or race. We cannot do it on our own or earn it; though many still try through worthless efforts. They are walking zombies (dead) without Christ.

> **Revelation 4:1** *After this I looked, and there before me was a door standing open in Heaven. And the voice I had first heard speaking to me like a Trumpet said, "Come up here and I will show you what must take place after this."*

The door standing open was an invite for John indicating a welcome, as in "let's talk I have something to show you." In order to show John what was going to take place, John needed to get out of the way to see the big picture of the magnitude that was to follow. So there was a simple subject change from writing to the seven churches, from the previous chapters. It also had gotten more personal from dictating these letters. Most Christians want to use this scripture as the bases for the Rapture. It just does not fit! There is no solid evidence or proof to support this reasoning. I wish it was true! But it is not, we will or have been going through some of the things written in this book.

I do not agree with pre-tribulation, mid-tribulation, or post-tribulation. I just simply believe in the tribulation period. There are other scholars that are starting to come around towards this direction. These terms are not actually found in the Bible. The Bible interprets itself, we do not interprets the Bible. We tend to get in trouble when we take the Bible out of context, and start adding or creating a different doctrine. The voice of a trumpet and the sound of a trumpet are two totally and completely different things (**Matthew 24:31**). In addition the Bible also tells us the "Last" trumpet, there must be at least more than one. Some believers want to also pinpoint that the word or name "church" is not mention after this verse. It is believed by many that it was simply a subject change from addressing the seven churches and now to another course of events coming soon. There is not one book in the Bible that only covers one particular subject; minus the short one chapter books. Instead of beating a dead horse, Jesus said what He needed to say to the churches and then moved on. The church is not really the main subject matter of the book of Revelation, but of the future course of events for planet earth, the bigger overall picture. We need to keep in mind John's primary focus was about the coming End Time events; signs, warnings and judgments (Wrath) on lost humanity, and the evil (**Romans 1:18; Chapter 2).**

Wrath is one of five things:

1. Wrath is just
2. Wrath is to be feared
3. Wrath is consistent
4. Wrath is love in action against sin
5. and Wrath is satisfied in Christ

We are also called by different titles or names, such as brothers or sisters, believers, followers, sheep, Christians, sons or daughters, kings and priests, adopted children and offspring. Church is just one name of many we are called as a fellowshipping bodily function. To put it in layman's terms; a Christian is any true follower of Jesus Christ, regardless of one's denomination. Though we are still in the church age, until the appointed time (the Rapture; aka the removal of the Holy Spirit and the church). This is also what is keeping Satan from an all-out war.

> *"And you know what restrains him now, so that in his time he will be revealed. For the mystery of lawlessness is already at work; only he who now restrains will do so until he is taken out of the way."* (**2 Thessalonians 2:6-7**)

Revelation 4:2-8 *"Immediately I was in the Spirit. And there was a throne set in heaven with One sitting on the throne! And He who* *sat there appeared like a jasper and a sardius stone. There was a rainbow around the throne, appearing like an emerald. Twenty-four thrones were around the throne. And I saw twenty-four elders sitting on the thrones, clothed in white garments. They had crowns of gold on their heads. Lightnings and thunderings and voices proceeded from the throne. Seven lamps of fire were burning before the throne, which are the seven Spirits of God. Before the throne was a sea of glass like crystal. In the midst of the throne, and around the throne, were four living creatures covered with eyes in front and in back. The first living creature was like a lion, the second living creature like a calf, the third living creature had a face like a man, and the fourth creature was like a flying eagle. The four living creatures had six wings each, and they were covered with eyes all around. All day and night, without ceasing, they were saying: "Holy, holy, holy, Lord God Almighty, who was, and is, and is to come."*

These stones are in reference to the twelve stones of the High Priest's breast plate, in **Exodus 28.** The first born of the tribe of Israel was Ruben, his stone happens to be jasper. The last born was Benjamin, his stone happens to be sardius. In other words, He on the throne was Jesus Christ, because He represents and is the first and the last, beginning and the end. [These 12 stones are also in the foundation of the New Jerusalem, **Revelation 21:10-21**].

Rainbows as we know them are semi-circles or half-circles. This rainbow is around the throne as a complete circle. This would represent the faithful promise of God, even when we are not. He is still full of grace. At the throne the promise is complete.

The 24 elders: most believe they are the 12 tribes of Israel in the Old Testament and the 12 Apostles in the New Testament.

The seven Spirits of God are: rest (peace, calm), wisdom, understanding, counsel, might (power, strength), knowledge, and fear (reverence) **Isaiah 11:2**.

These four living creatures can represent the four main foundations of the church and of our everyday life, since we are the church. These four living creatures told John to "Come and (or) See" after each of the first four Seals were opened (**6:1, 3, 5, 7**). In Ezekiel, he gave a clearer description, also that they were constantly being lifted up or going to a higher level, as they went in a direction. For more information about these four living creatures see **Ezekiel 1:5-28 & 3:13-14**.

In the Bible, numbers represents something. The number four represents earth or the physical realm as a whole. The Earth is made up of; Time, Energy, Space, & Matter. It has four seasons; Summer, Fall, Winter, & Spring. It has four directions; North, South, East, & West. There are four corners of the Earth and four phases of the Moon. There are also four divisions of the day; Morning, Noon, Evening, & Night. There are four acts of judgments; Sword, Famine, Wild Beast, & Pestilence. We also have four limbs.

The **Man** would represent Grace or Jesus. The term "Son of Man" is mentioned 82 times in the Gospels, such as in **Matthew 12:8; 20:28**. Grace and truth came through Jesus Christ (**John 1:17**).

The **Ox** would represent servanthood and humility. God blesses humility (**Micah 6:8**). Our highest calling is to be a servant (**2 Peter 1:1**). Our titles and positions do not matter, our identity is not in what we do; it is who we are (**Luke 12:15**). In order to go higher, we must go lower, everything is opposite in the Kingdom of God. If we want authority we must get under authority, **Job 5:11; Matthew 23:12**. Our highest prize is Jesus, everything else is useless and pointless (**Psalm 138:6**).

The **Eagle** would represent worship or abandonment (**Psalm 40:3**). Fully trusting in God and surrendering all control. We must give up total self to God. Genuine worship is yielding to All-Power **Genesis 22:15**, yielding to All-Knowledge **2 Samuel 15:26,** and yielding to All-Present **Joshua 5:13-14** God.

The **Lion** would represent prayer or war. It is happening all around us, we are at war whether we show up or not. If we do not show up in prayer; we will lose the battle (**Exodus 13:17**). A pursuit of a relationship with the Father **John 16:23-24**. A praise **Matthew 6:9**, prayer is about praise. A petition according to God's will (**1 John 5:14-15**). A protection **Matthew 6:13**, our enemy pretends to act like a lion (**1 Peter 5:8**). Jesus is the real lion. The way we do war is by developing a prayer relationship with God. A proclamation, to speak it out boldly (**Proverbs 6:2**).

Revelation 6:2 *The first Seal, I looked, and there before me was a White Horse! Its rider held a bow, and he was given a crown, and he rode out as a conqueror bent on conquest.*

Some believe that this represents the Antichrist while others say this could be the false prophet. I do not agree with either interpretation (even though I did at one time, years ago). It is just too vague to conclude this as an open and shut case, without something to go by. Some say that the person will be an influential leader with no use of weaponry. When I was younger I was told and believed that this was the Antichrist, without giving any thought to the matter. It wasn't until years later that it really did not make any sense to me. There were too many variables and improbabilities, as I started to look into it. So I commenced my own research. This horse can represent Catholicism (or religion/Popes), which still seemed doubtful and missing something; Even though this horseman seems to have the same kind of prideful arrogant spirit as the Pharisees. Again this would have to be much bigger than one individual person, even though the pope is well known worldwide. The other reason why I do not believe it is the antichrist or false prophet is simply because we are told who they are later in this book, as beasts.

Catholicism is a real religious belief in Jesus Christ, no different from all the other imperfect belief systems within God's churches. I am referring to all the manmade stipulations, bylaws, rituals and governing within its bodies of believers; not regarding or holding only to God's truths. We are still all very much human, that includes the popes and all the other leaders within these other church denominations. White would represents a false sense of holiness or righteousness that will mislead many from Christ. This would not be the case even in the Catholic belief, even though we may not agree with them. The Pope like other religious leaders is not perfect. There have been and will continue to be scandals within the denominations in general. During the history of the popes several of them sold out to secularism (persecution) for fear and for greed. Also, some of these popes were murdered or assassinated (or at least died under questionable circumstances).

Interfaithism is becoming a new tolerance of religious freedom or belief. They have held religious conferences as recently as 2010 (in Chicago). This organization supports all the groupings and manners of religion on the face of the earth, from Hinduism, Buddhism and Wickets, to black magic, sorceries, voodoos and homosexuality. The former British Prime Minister Tony Blair, of The Tony Blair Foundation and former U.S. President Bill Clinton supports Interfaithism. Their idea is that we should all just get along regardless of ones beliefs, background, culture or ethnic nationality, all for the greater good of mankind.

They have been pushing this belief tolerance in the United States, not at the college level or higher but at high schooler's and elementary school students. Which I thought was a bit odd since they are too young to vote or work in society. I wonder what kind of effect this will have on our next generation? At this time our elementary and high schools have mandated curriculums to teach the younger generation about Islam while denying Christian faith inside the schools. This also includes racial shaming and gender confusing curriculums. I think it is odd that it is okay to be from any other religion on the planet as long as it is not Christian based.

The "Separation of Church and State," has been completely taken out of context. The Founding Fathers' original ideas were to keep God in our schools as well as in our government. They knew the importance of keeping God in our society and to freely express our worship to Him alone. The Founders came from Europe under a religious oppression. They understood that one cannot dictate rules, when it is a personal relationship issue or relating to matters of the heart. This can usher in the one world religion. This must be finalized before a one world government can become possible.

Former U.S. President George W. Bush in a 2008 interview said that, "We all pray to the same God, we may have or use different means to get to God. Allah is just another name for God. Jesus (Christianity) is only one of many other ways to God." Wow, I was shocked when I heard him say that. No, there is only one way and one name to God, according to the Bible and that is through Jesus Christ alone, (**Acts 4:12**). Sorry to say there is no other name under heaven by which we are saved. We should be glad there is a "Way" to have access to God. I am not boasting or bragging because I am no better than you, it's the Bible.

The antichrist will mimic the Real Christ of 2000 plus years ago with a false sense of humility, unlike this prideful looking horseman. This rider appears to be more arrogant and prideful, similar to a Pharisees and Scribes in Jesus' time, including the crown. Some believe this rider will have authority over the second beast (**Revelation 13:11–17**). This horseman appears to me more arrogant, prideful, and might show more of a cold heart. This can also show something that can manipulate other people's thoughts and hearts.

In AD 800 Pope Leo III crowned Charlemagne, which birthed the (first government mixed religion) the "Holy Roman Empire," in 1806 it was resolved. In 2009 the "Revived Holy Roman Empire" was believed to officially reformed through the European Union (EU). This describes the vision statue in **Daniel 2:41**; the feet of clay representing religious rule and the iron represents government rule. They both will have a shared authority in this kingdom. Within the last hundred years every Pope has been favorable to a "One World Order" with the exception of one: Pope John Paul I, in 1978. He only reign for 33 days, after which he died of heart failure. His short lived reign may not have given him the opportunity to share his view points. And he was only 65 years old at the time, and never had any health problems nor was there any family history of such conditions. In fact the doctors gave him a perfect bill of health before taking office. His death has become at best questionable.

> **Revelation 6:4** *The second Seal, Another horse came out, a fiery Red Horse. Its rider was given power to take peace from the earth and to make men slaughter each other. To him was given a large sword.*

Through the centuries the one political party that has taken power and peace is socialist and or communism. In theory this could have been a good thing, but not at the hands of mortal beings. This was tried when the Colonies first landed in America and failed. Where everyone in society are required to work equally, fairly, and to share in the common good; but some refused out of laziness or were unable to work. There are no benefits to working hard when everyone gets the same rewards regardless. Their belief is to share the so called wealth while keeping the people poor because of motives of selfish greed and also to oppress them by removing their ability to protect themselves. Washington D.C. has been trying to push the "Share the Wealth" agenda.

From 1942 to 1962 communism went from about 10% to over 60% of the world's nations. Red also happens to represent this party's color. History shows how this horseman has been oppressing and slaughtering within their own countries. Human rights are taken away from them as the government fully controls their lives. This horseman has been growing stronger these last hundred years. Obama is said to be in favor of sharing the wealth, as in socialism. Now there are more and more democrats going further left towards socialism, to share the wealth and tax the rich ideas; it will not work.

> **Revelation 6:5-6** *"The third Seal, There before me was a Black Horse! Its rider was holding a pair of scales or balances in his hands. Then I heard what sounded like a voice among the four living creatures, saying "A quart of wheat for a day's wages & three quarts of barley for a day's wages, and do not damage or harm the oil and wine."*

Control the money, you control a country. In this sense the horseman can be represented as capitalism.

Around the early 1600's the Rothschild's institutionalized a money controlling company called the East India Company. Through the years it has changed names; the East India House, Chatham House, Royal Institution of International Affairs (Relations). And finally it came into the United States at the beginning of the last century. It was establishment in 1923 as the Council on Foreign Affairs also known as the "think tank." Most of, if not all of our key political leaders (Cabinet members in some cases and Presidents) have come from this Council on Foreign Relations (CFR). CFR is a private elite club rather than a company; it is not a government run agency.

To control a nation or to get them to do what you want, control and master their money, put them in debt. It was after the 1904 depression and the long battle over our monetary system made our country weak and finally the U.S. gave in to the idea of the Federal Reserve banking system. The United States has fought against this power from before the Revolutionary War (from 1781 until 1913), our founding fathers never wanted this and they knew it was wrong for our country. It is in our Constitution that the Federal Government was to make our money, not a company. But thanks to Mr. Paul Warburg a representative of the Rothschild's, along with six others that met on Jekyll Island in 1910 to establish this amendment, the Rothschild clan has pushed and made this happen. The Federal Reserve Bank (1913) was born and is not a part of our Federal Government; it is a privately owned company, based in Europe. They have many branches in the United States, but their main corporate office is overseas. It is now out of our control, something we will never get back. It was to be originally run by the Federal Government as per the United States Constitution section 8. In any event, it should have been the responsibility of the country, the ball was dropped when this was finally ratified while Congress was out on recess. It was illegally ratified while most of the lawmakers were out of town during a holiday shutdown in December and passed into law.

The Bilderberger group of less than a hundred of the richest people on the planet controls all the finances in the World, including the stock market and oil. We only know of a few, I will not name names. They are the major thinker, controlling even political leaders. They had a fit with President Trump, because they could not control him. The second election was stolen from him, which goes to show how evil and controlling they are. Their main focus is a globalization of monetary exchange and soon a cashless society as well as control of the world's overpopulation problem through created diseases (Covid), abortions, and wars. They too are a part of this group in question. They are a quiet, behind the scenes elite group, known to some as the real Puppet Masters. They have held secret meeting with key figures and leaders around the world. They are the ones in control, telling them what to do. They have even had power over some of our own presidents and other political leaders, which is clearly seen through the Biden administration; super high cost of everything and the lack of everything else. This shows how terrible the famine described here would be. Wheat and barley would sell at extravagant prices. People would spend an entire day's wages for just enough food to keep themselves alive. Even though the CFR and the Federal Reserve operate separate parts or functions, they mesh together as an overall bigger picture. President Trump had been driving these people crazy, because he could not be bought.

> **Revelation 6:8** *The fourth Seal. There before me was a Pale Ashe Greenish Horse! (black & bluish as if bruised). Its Rider was named Death, and Hades was following close behind him. They were given power over a fourth (1/4) of the earth to kill by the sword, famine & plague, and wild beasts of the earth.*

Most translations use pale and or ashe; but the original Greek word used according to Thayer's definition is "Chloros" which means 1) green 2) yellowish pale. Three other places that use chloros for green is, **Mark 6:39, Revelation 8:9; 9:4**. This passage is the only place where "pale" is used in place of green. The New Revised Standard uses pale green horse. This horse is not a solid color like the others; pale ashe is one color and greenish is another. Like a bruise (spotted or speckled) with a greenish tint. The wild beasts of the earth or fields, along with birds, dogs, scorpions, and snakes are commonly used as spiritual symbols referred as demons or evil spirits (**Jeremiah 15:3; Luke 10:19; Philippians 3:2**). This death horse many believe is in keeping with radical Islamism, though not all Muslims are bad. Again through the years they have killed millions of so called infidels (non-Muslims), or non-believers. One cannot compromise with this belief, unless you convert and reject Christ. Islamic color also happens to be green. Islamic radicals' beliefs are the biggest bruise on planet earth that we are facing. Hell is what follows close behind this belief, not the seventy-two virgins in paradise. The strongest religious and radical terrorist group in the world, are known through the Muslim community. Through their belief system of death, they highly honor and regard suicides and martyrdom for their causes is a high honor. Their pride goes far beyond the Japanese (culture) during WWII.

This type of religion is of violence and war, not of love and peace. Many theologians believe there is a connection with this verse and **Revelation 20:4**, that these beheadings are caused by this horseman's sword. If this is the case, the belief about a "guillotine" by others is totally false. Not only that, but the guillotine and or blade machine is unbiblical.

We can trace their history all the way to Ishmael in the book of Genesis (chapter 21, he will become a great nation). They did not start making a name for themselves until the A.D. 600's. In A.D. 610 Mohammad, their prophet; founded Islam. Since then they have invaded and conquered Egypt (639-642), Afghanistan (642-870), Georgia (645-735), North Africa (647-709) and southern Turkey (650).

They have attacked and pillaged Sicily several times (652-827); invaded and conquered Uzbekistan, Tajikistan & Kazakhstan (662-709), and Pakistan (664-712). They tried to siege Constantinople but failed (674-678).

In A.D. 691 the Dome of the Rock was built over Solomon's temple. During A.D. 700-1606 it dominated Sudan and southern Egypt, commenced persecutions of non-Muslims and those of interracial marriages. Between A.D. 711-750 they invaded and conquered Caucasus, Spain, Portugal, Gibraltar & Andorra (in A.D. 718 Spain and Portugal reclaimed their mainlands from the Muslims). Toulouse was besieged in A.D. 721.

In A.D. 732 France was able to prevent Muslim advancement towards Paris. From A.D. 827 to 902 they attacked and invaded numerous times and conquered southern Italy's cities of Amalfi, Gaeta, Naples, Salerno & Sicily. During A.D. 846-1830 as the Barbary Pirates started attacking ships at sea, stealing their cargoes and selling the crew into slavery in the North Africa region. In A.D. 982 they defeated Germany's army and allies in the battle of Stilo, in Italy. In A.D. 1056 they forced removal, expelling over 300 Christians from Jerusalem. In A.D. 1063 they defeated the king of Aragon in the battle at Graus, Spain. From A.D. 1071-1091 they invaded and conquered Anatolia (modern Turkey). In A.D. 1091-1099 Christians, under the guide of (the first) Crusaders halted the Muslim advancement on Vienna; preventing them from conquering all of Europe, allowing Christians to return to the Holy Land (there were a total of nine crusades).

In A.D. 1139 Portugal's army defeated Muslim attack. In A.D. 1187 the Muslims invades and reconquers Jerusalem. In A.D. 1192 invades and conquers Delhi. In A.D. 1195 they defeated a Christian army at Alarcos, Spain. In A.D. 1229 the Muslims gave up Jerusalem in exchange for Europeans to leave Egypt. In A.D. 1244 they invaded and retook Jerusalem. From A.D. 1260-1300 they counterattacked and fought off East Asian Mongols. From A.D. 1299-1453 attacked and defeated the Byzantine Empire. During A.D. 1332-1853 the Muslims (Ottoman Turks) fought against the Albanians.

From 1350-1699 they fought against Bulgaria. The Muslims invaded and conquered Serbia and Bosnia from A.D. 1380-1389. Invaded in A.D. 1380-1521 south Philippians and forced them to convert.

The Ottoman Turks (Muslims) invaded and conquered the Republic of Venice from A.D. 1423-1503, Hungary from A.D. 1439-1526 and Indonesian, Archipelago from A.D. 1441-1491. In A.D. 1441 attacked Poland but sustained heavy losses and withdrew to reconsider advancing onto central Europe. Repeatedly attacked Greece but failed to conquer it from A.D. 1444-1853. In A.D. 1453 Constantinople was again invaded and conquered. From A.D. 1453-1683 invaded and conquered the Balkans. In A.D. 1496 Spain and Portugal expels the Muslim invaders from the Iberian Peninsula.

From A.D. 1500-1683 a jihad war breaks out against Austria and Hungary. In A.D. 1522 they invaded and conquered the Isle of Rhodes. In A.D. 1529 there was a failed attempt to siege Vienna. From A.D. 1568-1570 they attacked Russia but were held back and loss ground. From A.D. 1620-1621 attacked Poland which was a standoff. From A.D. 1645-1669 they invaded and conquered Crete.

Again from A.D. 1672-1676 Ottoman attacked Poland it was still a standoff. In A.D. 1683 again laid siege to Vienna Austria, a failed attempt. From A.D. 1683-1918 the Ottoman Empire started to decline, rebellion started in most of their conquered territories;

they were unable to conquer more territories or to finance their wars; defeated during WWI.

In A.D. 1795 they invaded and pillaged Tbillisi. In A.D. 1798 the French defeated the Muslims at the battle of the Pyramids in Egypt. From 1860-1865 they massacred about 10,000 Christians in Lebanon. From A.D. 1894-1916 they waged an all-out war against Armenians murdering 1.5 million; pillaged and destroyed 568 churches, converted 282 into Mosques, tortured and killed 21 preachers and 170 priests for refusing to convert to Islam. From A.D. 1914-1918 the Ottoman Empire ended under the rule of Britain, and French sanction later U.N. mandate. In 1948 the Jews are declared a Jewish State (Israel); Muslims began waging war against Israel, mandate rule expires for Palestine. In 1950 U.N. mandate expires in all other countries, Muslims resume their wars and conquest worldwide. 1967 borders are extended in counterattack for Israel during six day war with Muslims. In 1973 Egyptian and Syrian Muslims attack Israel (Yom Kippur) killed 2,200 and wounded 3,000 Israelites; some borders were lost. In 1974 Muslims slaughtered 1,000 Christians in Cyprus. In 1979 they kidnapped 52 U.S. Embassy workers in Tehran, Iran for 444 days. From 1981-1989 the Muslims waged war against Russia in Afghanistan ending their occupation. In 1983 a suicide car bomber attacked the French and U. S. military base in Lebanon and killed 78 French soldiers and 241 U. S. marines. In 1996 Osama Bin Ladin declares a holy war against the U. S. and the U.K. In 1998 he and the Islamic leaders declare a holy war against the U.S. and Israel. Also in 1998 a suicide bomber attack's the U. S. Embassy in Kenya and in Tanzania killing 214 and wounded over 5,000 people. In 2000 the USS Cole was bombed killing 17 and wounded 39 sailors. In 2001 (September 11th) four aircrafts were hijacked destroying both towers of the World Trade Center in New York City and parts of the Pentagon killing 3,017 and wounded 6,291. In 2002 they bombed the resort in Bali, Indonesia killing 202, wounded 209.

In 2003 they bombed two synagogues in Turkey killing 57 and wounded 700.

In 2004 they bombed a train in Madrid, Spain killing 191 and wounded 1,800. Also in 2004, 1,100 hostages were taken in Russia they killed 300 including 186 children. In 2005 they bombed a train and bus station in U. K. killing 52 and wounded 700 people. In 2006 they invaded and conquered Somalia. In 2008 they attacked a hotel in Mumbai, India killing 173 and wounded 308. In 2009 they forced expulsion of all relief agencies from Darfur region of Sudan, their intent was to starve to death 1,000,000 non-Muslims. Also in 2009 a devout Muslim murdered 13 and wounded 29 military people at Fort Hood, Texas; another incident almost succeeded in blowing up Northwest Airlines flight 253 and killing 289 passengers on Christmas Day.

In 2010 another devout Muslim attempted to detonate a car bomb at Times Square in New York City.

In 2011 they burned 50 churches and murdered 461 Christian in Nigeria.

I apologize for putting you through their history (dates only includes from 600-2011 A.D.), but I did it to prove a couple of points. Number one, we cannot cohabitate and secondly we cannot negotiate or compromise with this dark sickening evil. You and I will never be able to change their mindset, nor will we ever be able to befriend them. At least not on our own, only God can do that. Their history is so full of bloodshed, violence, attacks, invasions, pillaging, conquering and the like. That is all they ever knew.

The Shariah law allows them to purposely lie to anyone to gain favor, position, and control over. It also allows them to justify killing or murdering anyone that stands in their way, or seems to be a threat to their way of life. They are extremely dangerous and cannot be trusted. They do play on human passions to gain control. Again, there is a huge difference between an Islamic radical Muslim terrorist and a religious Muslim. From the breaking of this Seal until Armageddon (completion) this Horseman will have control of a fourth of the earth.

Some believe in the ISMs, which makes a little more sense from a harmony, unity, and orderly God. This belief would go hand in hand with Catholicism as the white horse, Communism as the red horse, Capitalism as the black horse, and Islamism as the greenish horse. Yet again I see a possible error within these ISMs. Secularism or even Materialism might fit better the white horse. Or possibly even

Paganism. What better way to be bent on conquering than through our minds, thoughts, and our way of thinking.

Both the Antichrist and the false prophet will be behind and control with all authority these two types of "systems" known as beast number one and beast number two. These riders will be a part of the bigger systems, or subsystems. These four horsemen are much bigger than just individual people, but they are spirits, subsystems to the main whole system. In **Zechariah 6:5-8**, they are referred as the four spirits of heaven, going out from the presences of our Lord of the whole world. They were sent in different directions. Another translation uses winds instead of spirit, similar reference in **Genesis 2:7** which also refers to the breathe of God, entering into man. These four riders will and have captured the hearts and minds of men, so these horsemen are controlling thoughts, if we allow such a thing.

The fourth horse in Zechariah is described as dapple or speckled. These four spirits are eagerly patrolling the earth. The white horse Secularism or Paganism can easily represent every false fake religions, black magic, and cults, along with everything that separates, preoccupies, and keeps us from our Creator. This would include idoltery. The question at hand is, are you growing, maturing and renewing your mind daily? It is not enough to just go to or have churchy stuff and all the feel good things. I call this motion sickness. What good are we if we are not changing and growing towards Godliness, Holiness or Righteousness? This is why I have come to believe, it is not the antichrist or false prophet, but what we worship and place above the one true God. Whatever you spend more time with has become your master and god; as in technology. It is our own personal god what we cherish within us. This is the same concept with the other three horse riders; they all want power.

The second spirit, Communism or socialism, has complete authority over the lower class poor, there is no middle class. This is called oppression, slavery (human trafficking) and abuse of humanity.

The third spirit Capitalism goes back beyond Wall Street and the stock market exchange. The greed for all manner of riches that seeks honor and high positions, with no regards towards fellow mankind.

The fourth spirit Islamism, hates anyone that disagrees with their belief. They will continue to fight those that are against them and stand in their way for a one world dominating ethnic group. So these are four subsystems from the overall bigger picture.

The four horsemen are thought to symbolize powerful forces that will harm people: brute militarism, war and violence, famine and food shortages, death and hell. This is a picture of a powerful destructive force of military might and conquest. These three riders form of a conquering group here; violence, famine, and death are evil and brutal.

Can these powerful spiritual forces simply be inside of us causing our thoughts and emotions to move in an inhuman way? Take a good close look around in our world today at the manifestation of evil and the struggle between good and evil.

The majority of the churches believe that the White Horseman is either the antichrist or the false prophet. If this were the case the other three horsemen must also be a person. God is not a messy God, nor does He just throw things together haphazardly or helter-skelter. It must systematically fit in an orchestrated manner. They all must come or be from the same origin or type.

Revelation 6:9-11 *"The fifth Seal, I saw under the altar the souls of those who had been slain because of the Word of God and the Testimony they had maintained. They called out in a loud voice, "How long, Sovereign Lord, Holy and True, until You judge the inhabitants of the earth and avenge our blood?" Then each of them was given white robe, and they were told to wait a little longer, while until the number of their follow servants and brothers who were to be killed as they had been was completed."*

Imagery is reminiscent of the altar of sacrifice, which stood in the temple's outer court. This altar has a trough under it to catch the blood of sacrificed animals. These victims' souls are poured out under the altar are believers who were slain because of their witnessing. God allows certain things to occur, including the deaths of His servants, which furthers His ultimate purposes. The blood of martyrs is the seed of the church, meaning non-Christians saw their faith and courage and then decided to convert, causing the church to grow. Since there is a number that will be killed shows that God is ultimately in control. Some believe that this may have to do with the "Holocaust" victims during WWII. I simply believe they were possibly all the martyred saints of the past, present, and soon future. They will show up again at the end of this book.

> **Revelation 6:12-17** *"The sixth Seal, There was a great earthquake. The sun turned black like sackcloth made of goat hair, the whole moon turned blood red, and the stars in the sky fell to the earth, as late figs drop from a fig tree when shaken by a strong wind. The sky receded like a scroll, rolling up, and every mountain and island was removed from its place. The kings of the earth, the princes, the generals, the rich, the mighty, and every slave and every free man (all of the inhabitants) hid in caves and among the rocks of the mountains. They called to the mountains and the rocks, "Fall on us and hide us from the face of Him who sits on the Throne and from the WRATH of the Lamb! For the great day of their WRATH has come, and who can stand?"*

Some disagree and see a literal reading while others a poetic description. This describes literal calamities such as war and famine. However others say this symbolizes God's final judgment using images familiar in the Old Testament. Or the final judgment at Christ's coming. It will bring wrath on the wicked and reward to the faithful. Chapter seven focuses on those whom God's *Wrath* is spared.

Earthquakes that have been recorded since 1900 have shown a steady pace; until 2000-2009, which shows a spike. The average major earthquakes between 1900 and 2000 as per decade, average 43. As per each decade around the world reaching at 5.5 plus on the Richter scale:

1900 to 1909= 36,	1910 to 1919= 26,
1920 to 1929= 28,	1930 to 1939= 40,
1940 to 1949= 41,	1950 to 1959= 49,
1960 to 1969= 61,	1970 to 1979= 49,

1980 to 1989= 41,   1990 to 1999= 62,

2000 to 2009= 425,   2010 to 2020= 278.

This is the first time the word "Wrath" is mentioned twice. Yet God is not the one speaking about His actual Wrath, not until later. The Wrath is coming from the mouths of the inhabitants of the earth, N*ot* God's mouth. This leads many to think that this is the starting point for God's Wrath and the reasoning for the Rapture to happen at this point in time. This belief is totally false. It would still not make sense why the word Wrath is continually mentioned four more times later on. This tells me that apparently the first five seals went unnoticed. Now it becomes more noticeable during natural disasters. This does not include: blizzards, heat waves, tsunamis, cyclones, hurricanes and tornados that have also increased through recent years as well. His birth pains are there, we just got too callous and numb to sense or notice.

The United States has been hit with more hurricanes and tornados in the last eighty years than in any other part of our history. Could this be caused by the removal of God from our nation? We are presently a divided and torn country.

John relates the stars falling from the sky like figs from a fig tree, late in the season. Most of these stars won't necessarily all land on the earth. In fact a lot of them either burnt out in space or do fall into space, but miss the earth altogether. When was the last time you really actually looked at the night skies? There just doesn't seem to be as many stars in the sky, like there was when I was growing up.

The moon turning blood red has happened irregularly throughout the years. But to happen in a set of four, known as tetrads is very rare. It does not happen very often, but each time impacts the nation of Israel. There have only been four sets of four in the last 600 years, three of them were all within the last eighty-five years. They appeared in sets of four and within a two year time span. Starting during the Passover (March/ April) and during the feast of Tabernacles (September/ October) of that same year, this would follow the same pattern the following year, ending at the feast of Tabernacles.

The first one was in 1493-94 during the Spanish inquisition; which attacked and expelled (exiled) the Jewish people from the rest of the world, which gave birth to a new continent known as the Americas (Christopher Columbus was Jewish).

The next set occurred in 1949-50, when up until the rebirth of the State of Israel on the 14th of May 1948, there has been no place they could call home for over three thousand years as they continued to fight for their independence from the surrounding Islamic counties. They fought four wars during this short amount of time; which ended with signed truces between Egypt, Syria, Jordan and Lebanon, establishing Israel's borders.

The third tetrad happened in 1967-68, during the Six Day War of June 5-10, 1967, the same enemies rose up against them to try to destroy them once again. God was giving Israel the greatest victory, to take and possess their original promise land mass for His chosen people. Israel held their position and gained most of her original promised land. This would have included the Dome of the Rock, but they failed to go after it and stopped short of actually possessing everything that was theirs. Israel has more than tripled its land from that war. Now, at this time Israel took control of Jerusalem (their Holiest site) as their new Capital and Judea known as the occupied territory aka the West Wall. They lost the southern portion back to the Egyptians but also gained a little during the 1973 Yom Kippur War. During the Camp David Accords of the 1978 peace agreement Israel gave back Egypt's land boarder by 1982, something they should have never done since it was a covenant between God and Abraham. Israel shrunk back down to its present day size.

The last Blood Moon was in 2014-15 and Israel is now facing another battle with her enemies. God's favor is and always will be with this nation. Fighting with them is like picking a fight with God; you will lose. Each time Israel gains favor with God and gains a victory somehow. Unlike zodiac signs, God gives and uses signs to mark seasons (**Genesis 1:14**). Also in fulfilling His prophecies, such as the Star that gave direction towards the birth of the Jewish Messiah and sacrificial King to the world.

I believe this Blood Moon may had something to do with President Donald Trump and the favor of Israel again. He moved the U.S. Embassy from Tel Aviv to Israel's capital, Jerusalem in 2018 on the seventieth anniversary of the establishment of Israel. All the past presidents said they would do that, but failed to commit. This was a huge deal. This President has and done more for Israel than any of the other administrations to date. Other administrations more or less turned their backs on Israel.

> **Revelation 7:1-2** *"I saw four angels standing at the four corners of the earth, holding back the four winds of the earth to prevent any wind from blowing on the land or on the sea or on any tree. Then I saw another angel coming up from the east, having the seal of the Living God. He called out in a loud voice to the four angels who had been given power to harm the land and the sea."*

During Old Testament times often the winds followed the judgments of God. At this point it would be a whole lot windier if these four angels did not prevent the full force of God's judgment to fall. They were minimizing the impending doom for its appointed time. Since these four angels were at the four corners of the earth stopping the four winds, it shows that God's judgment will come upon the entire planet. Some have thought this was meaning to take away the breeze or some lack of oxygen to sustain human life or increased in humidity. This type of thing would not happen until the Vials. Since a lot has happened, the wind of God's judgment is in the air. His Wrath is just around the corner!

Some theologians have thought that these four angels had something to do with the four horsemen. The four angels were keeping spiritual tight reigns on the winds from spreading out of control. Some other scholars view this as what Paul wrote in Second Thessalonians; that which is restraining the wide spread of evil as long as the church and Holy Spirit are still on the earth.

> **Revelation 7:3-8** *"Do not harm the land or the sea or the trees until we put a seal on the foreheads of the servants of our God. Then I heard the number of those who were sealed: 144,000 from all the*

tribes of Israel. From the tribe of Judah 12,000 were sealed, from the tribe of Reuben 12,000, from the tribe of Gad 12,000, from the tribe of Asher 12,000, from the tribe of Naphtali 12,000, from the tribe of Manasseh 12,000, from the tribe of Simeon 12,000, from the tribe of Levi 12,000, from the tribe of Issachar 12,000, from the tribe of Zebulun 12,000, from the tribe of Joseph 12,000, from the tribe of Benjamin 12,000."

As believers we are well known as sheep in the Bible. But we are also known as "trees" (**Psalm 1:1-3**, **37:35**; **Ezekiel 31:3-14**; **Mark 8:23-25**; **Luke 6:43-44**). So we are either a healthy strong green tree planted by the river which is the Word of God. Or we are a feeble weak brown tree planted in a dry desert place. The Gentile believers are put on hold until the Jewish servants of God receive their Seal.

The angel yells out, Stop what you're doing; do not go any further. At this time there seems to be a brief pause just before the last Seal is to usher in the seven sets of Trumpets. So before continuing on, the 144,000 from the twelve tribes of Israel must be sealed. These are considered by some as God's remnants. Notice that these twelve tribes mentioned here are NOT in birth order by seniority NOR are they from the original tribes. Such as Manasseh was not one of the tribes but Joseph's son and Dan is completely missing.

The names of people in the Old Testament had meaning or always meant something, there was always a purpose to the person's name or the whys behind it. For example, Jabez means hardship or pain (**I Chronicles 4:9**). So God did not just throw these names out there in some old haphazardly way.

The list of the tribes of Jacob (Israel) in order of birth from oldest to youngest from **Genesis 29:32-35**; **30:5-12, 17-20, 22-24**; **35:16-18,** and their meanings:

Names	Meanings	Birth Mothers
Reuben	The Lord has looked upon my affliction	Leah

Simeon	The Lord has heard (me) that I was unloved (hated)	Leah
Levi	This time my husband will be joined (attached) to me	Leah
Judah	I will praise the Lord	Leah
Dan	God has vindicated (judged) me, He has heard my voice	Bilhah
Naphtali	With (because of) great wrestling have I wrestled and I have won	Bilhah
Gad	How (given good) fortunate, a troop comes	Zilpah
Asher	Happy am I, I will be called blessed	Zilpah
Issachar	God has given me my reward (purchased/wages)	Leah
Zebulun	God has given me a good gift, He will dwell with me	Leah
Joseph	God has taken away my reproach, Lord will add to me another son	Rachel
Benjamin	Son of my pain, son of my right hand (side)	Rachel

Genesis 41:51-52

| Manasseh | For God said He has made me forget all my toil | Asenath |
| Ephraim | For God has caused me to be fruitful in the land of my affliction | |

The list in order from **Revelation 7:5-8**, is Not in order of birth, missing Dan (which comes at a later date) & Ephraim:

1. Judah (4)-   I will **praise the Lord**

2. Reuben (1)-   The **Lord** has **looked upon my affliction**

3. Gad (7)-   How **given good** (fortune) **fortunate**

4. Asher (8)-   **Happy** (blessed) **am I**

5. Naphtali (6)-   **Because of great wrestling**, I have won

6. Manasseh (13)-   He **(God)** has **made me forget** all my toils (troubles)

7. Simeon (2)-   The **Lord has heard** (hears), I was hated

8. Levi (3)-   He will be **attached to me** (joined to)

9. Issachar (9)-   God has **purchased me** (my reward)

10. Zebulun (10)-   He will **dwell**(s) **with me**, (a good gift)

11. Joseph (11)-   Taken away my reproach, **will add to me**

12. Benjamin (12)- Son of my pain, **son of my right hand**

By putting each name's meaning in order, this is what that scripture is saying:

> *"I will praise the Lord for He has looked on me and given me good fortune. Happy am I, because of my wrestling, God is making me to forget my troubles. God hears me and is attached to me. He has purchased me a dwelling place and will add to me the Son of His right hand."*

One of the sons of Jacob was a youngster by the name of Dan, which means "judge or to be judged." He was the son of Rachel's handmaid Bilhah (**Genesis 35:25**). Dan became the ancestor of one of the twelve tribes of Israel, the name YEHOVAH God gave to Jacob after wrestling with him (**Genesis 32:28**).

> Jacob, when he was growing old, prophesied of Dan, "*Dan will provide justice for his people as one of the tribes of Israel. Dan will be a serpent by the roadside, a viper along the path that bites the horse's heels, so that its rider tumbles backward. I look for your deliverance, O Lord*" (**Genesis 49:16-18**). The King James Version has this last verse, "*I have waited for thy salvation, O Lord.*"

A serpent, when it slithers and crawls, leaves a trail or track in the sand. Even so the tribe of Dan would leave signs or "waymarks" showing where it had journeyed. They tended to leave their "name" behind as an identifying sign! We read in Joshua:

> "*But the Danites had difficulty taking possession of their territory, so they went up and attacked Leshem, took it, put it to the sword and occupied it. They settled in Leshem and NAMED IT DAN after their forefather*" (**Joshua 19:47**).

For some reason, as this prophecy states, Dan must "wait" for Yehovah's salvation—even longer than the other tribes. In the book of Revelation, when the Messiah tells the apostle John that he will choose 144,000 special servants from the twelve tribes of Israel (**Revelation 7:1-8**), and chooses 12,000 out of each tribe, it is interesting to note that he gives Joseph a double portion—a portion for Ephraim (Joseph) and a portion for his brother Manasseh (**Revelation 7:6, 8**)

The tribe of Dan still had not settled down and occupied their "inheritance" in Canaan (**Judges 18-2**), so they sent five warriors forth to explore the land. They found a Levitical priest of the Lord in the house of a man named Milcah, and enquired whether Yehovah God would bless their endeavor. He said yes. They journeyed forth and found a city, Laish, dwelling securely and prosperously, went back and urged their tribe to attack it, and 600 Danites sallied forth. But on their way, they set up camp in a place they named Mahaneh Dan (**Judges 18:12**) and then came to Milcah's house again.

> *"The six hundred Danites, armed for battle, stood at the entrance to the gate. The five men who had spied out the land went inside and took the carved image, the ephod, the other household gods and the cast idols while the priest and the six hundred armed men stood at the entrance to the gate. When the men went into Milcah's house and took the carved image, the ephod, the other household gods, and the cast idol, the priest said to them, 'What are you doing?' They answered him, 'Be quiet! Don't say a word! Come with us and be our father and priest. Isn't it better that you serve a tribe and clan in Israel as priest rather than just one man's household?' Then the priest was glad"* (**Judges 1:16-20***).

The tribe of Dan was the first tribe of Israel to plunge into paganism idolatry! Over the centuries, they have become steeped in idolatry and image worship—so much so that they will be slow to repent of their sins and to come out of the prevalent Endtime idolatry of Roman Catholicism, which numbers over 900 million adherents around the world today.

Characteristics of Dan

Dan was born to Bilhah about 1737 B.C. (**Genesis 30:1-9**). He was a rambunctious youth, and multiplied greatly in tribal descendants during the sojourn of the Israelites in Egypt (**Exodus 1:7-9, 12**). When Moses led the children of Israel out of Egypt, in about 1483 B.C., the tribe of Dan which accompanied him numbered some 62,700 men old enough to make war, 20 years old and upward (**Numbers 1:38-39**). Dan descendants out numbered Manasseh, the son of Joseph by almost 2 to 1, and outnumbered the children of Ephraim about 3 to 1.

When Moses gave his final blessings to the children of Israel, he said, "And of Dan he said, Dan is a lion's whelp: he shall leap from Bashan" (**Deuteronomy 33:22**). Dan would be a vigorous, warlike, with a tribe of warriors. He would not sit solitary, and be content but would "leap" forth.

In the book of Judges, we learn another trait of this tribe. In the song of Deborah and Barak, during the time of the Judges, the song asks, "Why did Dan remain in ships?" (**Judges 5:17**) Or, "Dan abode in ships." The tribe of Dan was a mighty sea-faring tribe, which loved to sail the seas.

Dan—A Serpent's Trail

In the division of Palestine among the twelve tribes of Israel, after the Exodus from Egypt, Dan received his portion in the very north. As Dan was unable to secure and conquer much of its inheritance due to spiritual weaknesses, they felt hemmed in and constrained to migrate and conquer elsewhere, which is one reason they captured Laish and renamed it "Dan." Their inheritance was near the cities of Tyre and Sidon, famous home ports of the Phoenicians. Dan, who "abode in ships," made common concourse with the Phoenicians, intermarried with them, and established colonies throughout the Mediterranean region.

In the downfall of the northern kingdom of Israel in 718-721 B.C., the inland portion of the tribe of Dan was carried into captivity with the other tribes composing the northern kingdom, led by Ephraim. This portion of Dan was taken into captivity beyond the Euphrates River, into Assyria, and when the Assyrian Empire fell in the seventh century B.C., they migrated through the Caucasian Pass, just north of the Caucasus. This was known as the land of the "Sarmatians," and the pass was called the "Sarmatian Gate." The name Sarmatia was obviously derived from the name Samaria, which was the capital of the northern kingdom of Israel. These people called themselves the Scoloti, but the Greeks called them Sythians. These people continued migrating to the northwest of Europe and eventually many of them settled in the British Isles, and are the "Scots" of today. The chief tribe of the northern kingdom of Israel was Ephraim, the youngest son of Joseph. Even after Ephraim was carried away into captivity, and never returned, Yehovah's heart still yearned for him. Yehovah God said through the prophet Jeremiah:

*"Is not Ephraim my dear son, the child in whom I delight? Though I often speak against him, I still remember him. Therefore my heart yearns for him, declares the Lord. Set Up Road Signs, Put Up Guideposts. Take note of the highway, the road that you take. Return, O Virgin Israel, return to your towns. How long will you wander, O unfaithful daughter" (**Jeremiah 31:20-22**)?"*

As the Israelites migrated through Europe, they fulfilled this prophecy, and left "Road signs" and "Guideposts" along the way, so that we could trace their route! The chief tribe to do this was Dan, because of their proclivity to leave the name of their ancestor "Dan" everywhere they went.

Denmark, the name of the modern country in Europe north of Germany, means, literally, "Dan's mark." Its people are called "Danes." In fact, because at one time Denmark ruled all the surrounding region, the whole region took its name from them the Scan(DIN)-avian peninsula! Clearly, here are remnants of the people of Dan, who migrated westward overland from the Caucasus to their present location in northern Europe!

"A Covenant People"

*In Isaiah 49, a prophecy for the End Time, Yehovah God says, "Listen to me, you islands; hear this, you distant nations" (**Isaiah 49:1**). This is a message to the scattered nations of the northern kingdom of Israel. Yehovah Says to them, (**vs 8**) "In the time of my favor I will answer you, and in the day of salvation I will help you; I will keep you and will make you TO BE A COVENANT FOR THE PEOPLE, to restore the land and to reassign its desolate inheritances…"*

What the Future Holds

The tribe of Dan, more than any other of the "lost ten tribes of Israel," left its "signature" wherever it migrated or journeyed. It did so by the unique method of naming rivers, mountains, lakes, villages, towns, bays, and cities after the name of their ancestor; Dan.

Because of this attitude, the modern descendants of Dan are the most wayward and idolatrous and far from Yehovah God of all the tribes.

Therefore, Jacob declared, Dan prophetically has no say, unlike the other tribes of Israel: Yehovah God says of His people Israel, including the tribe of Dan:

> *"Though you were ruined and made desolate and your land laid waste, now you will be too small for your people, and those who devoured you will be far away. The children born during your bereavement will yet say in your hearing, 'This place is too small for us; give us more space to live in.' Then you will say in your heart, 'Who bore me these? I was bereaved and barren; I was exiled and rejected. Who brought these up? I was left all alone, but these—where have they come from?'... Then you will know that I am the Lord; those who hope in me will not be disappointed"* (**Isaiah 49:19-23**).

SIDE BAR: For the record these twelve tribes are not the original tribes of Israel. According to **Genesis 29:30** the original tribes are as follows; Reuben, Simeon, Levi, Judah, **DAN**, Naphtali, Gad, Asher, Issachar, Zebulun, Joseph and Benjamin. Dan was removed from the list and Manasseh, Joseph's first born was added to the list. In the book of Numbers chapter one the twelve tribes are changed to; Reuben, Simeon, Judah, Dan, Naphtali, Gad, Asher, Issachar, Zebulun, **EPHRAIM, MANASSEH** and Benjamin. Levi was removed from the list and was placed as God's (inheritance) priestly tribe; they were given their portions from the other tribes in the form of tithes and offerings. Joseph was removed from the list all together; he was also considered Jacob's favorite son. In so his name was dropped and was given double portions through his two sons, Ephraim and Manasseh. Now in this chapter Joseph was added back as one of the original twelve tribes while Dan was removed. Ephraim was dropped from the list where Manasseh stayed on this list, as the first born son. Some believe that since Joseph is again a part of the twelve tribes, that Joseph and Ephraim are one and the same. Or that they would somehow share the same portion within the tribes. During this type of culture it is considered customary and normal for the eldest or leading tribe (son) to bore or carry on the father's (Joseph) name. Joseph the first born from Rachel was the favorite and received a double portion.

In regards to the tribe of Dan, many scholars believe they were guilty of gross idolatry. They were known for even stealing false images used in religious rituals and ceremonies. They even took over a town in one of their raids and turned it into a place of cultic immoral activities. They were also believed to be the first organized "idolatry" in ancient Israel, as well as the longest in duration. This went on for nearly 500 years, until they were put into captivity (**Judges 18:14-31**). According to Jewish tradition it is believed that Dan was the first to follow Jeroboam into his sin of idolatry. In Jewish modern literature the term "Dan" is normally used to represent idolatry. Dan completely rejected God's commandments and laws for thousands of years; substituting the genuine true God for less. But, there is still hope for Dan, they are not completely lost. They will just have to wait for their salvation. Dan is mentioned first in the apportioning of the land (**Ezekiel 48:1**) during the soon coming millennium.

> **Revelation 8:1-5** *"The SEVENTH Seal, there was silence in Heaven for half (1/2) an hour. I saw seven angels standing before God, to them were given the seven Trumpets. Another angel, who had a golden censer, came and stood at the altar. He was given much incense to offer with the prayers of all the saints, on the golden altar before the throne. The smoke of the incense, together with the prayers of the saints, went up before God from the angel's hand. Then the angel took the censer, filled it with fire from the altar, and hurled it on the earth: and there came peals of thunder, rumblings, flashes of lightning and an earthquake."*

This could be poetic saying this was a long silence in heaven. In the Bible this often comes before or with God's judgments or ushering in something new. There was about 430-450 years of silence between the Old and New Testaments. There was also about 150 years between Jonas' sent message to Nineveh from God and their eventual destruction. This dramatic pause signals that the judgment to come is going to be just as long and dramatic. This silence could prepare people to hear (yet doubtful the coming trumpets.) Some noted as regarding this silence as suppression and the lack of published individual Bibles. Or the warring crusaders claim to God's service, during the Middle Ages. They did not start allowing church members their own published Bibles until the early/ mid 1600's. They had a lot of government, state run churches that were under the rule of political leaders. Bibles were only reserved for the clergies up to this point. Regardless, God does use calm before as the coming storm draws nearer. Eventually it is finalized at His Wrath to come. This Seal being broken would be the introduction or the beginning of the next phase to come.

In the Old Testament to modern times incense and prayer have been associated with each other. This image shows them both going heavenward into the very throne room of God, emphasizing power in prayers. This show the importance of prayers and that God knows every one of them. Often we might feel that God does not hear our prayers or that they just do not seem to penetrate high enough to God. This also shows the longevity of the Seals that finally ends at Armageddon. The angel throws the censer down to earth since there is (or will be) no more need or use for prayers.

CHAPTER THREE

THE TRUMPETS SOUNDED

THE SEVEN TRUMPETS: a short time period ending at Armageddon. Like all musical instruments the notes sound and echo as it slowly dies out. Each note can overlap one another, like unto a medley. So, all of the trumpets would have to be sounded closer to the end times, within the last century or so. These Trumpets can be classified as still warning signs or judgments to the End Time events. As the seven angels prepared themselves to sound these Trumpets; again they never left Heaven so they were never sent as Messengers of God's Wrath of judgment. We will not be able to hear these Trumpets through our physical ears because God is Spirit **(John 4:24)**, but possibly with spiritual ears or this can simply be implied symbolism.

All these Trumpets were or are blown while still in Heaven. To simplify this, how would an individual know they were being evicted unless they were given the information. Or if they were hired or fired from a job unless someone was sent to communicate the official decree, order, or message. There will be no sense or need to do guess work regarding God's Wrath. At this point everything is starting to pick up speed.

Revelation 8:7 *"The FIRST angel sounded his Trumpet, hail and fire mixed with blood was hurled down upon the earth. A third of the earth was burned up, a third of the trees burned, and all the green grass was burned up."*

In Bible times trumpets were used to warn people and to gather them before battles, national emergencies or celebrations. Trumpets came to symbolize warning judgment and a call for repentance, feasts or for an emergency. Paul linked a trumpet call with Christ's return (**I Thessalonians 4:16**).

Some believe that the first Trumpet sounded during WWI (1914-1918). The weaponry used became different from all the other past conflicts, such as improved flamethrowers, trench mortars and mines. WWI also introduced poisonous gas bombs (biological chemical agents) and plane warfare.

Scorched earth policy is a known warfare tactics; it simply means, if the enemy is advancing, to burn and destroy "everything"; land, buildings, trees, livestock, plants, animals, vehicles, crops. This has been a normal policy in any art of war. The third can refer to a time period or area, but I believe it could be an overall total. Though this policy was a common practice in the past, it became more widely enforced and used during WWI. This war killed roughly 8.2 million people, at this point in time no amount of war killings ever superseded a million. It was never heard of in any of the past conflicts until now. John could have also seen sparks or red hot artillery fires from cannons, tanks and guns, instead of hail. He never said it came from heaven, we could assume since that is where hail comes from, if it did. I believe he would have said so. We can add hail and flame throwers upon the earth mixed with blood. It was a new type of warfare that John was describing.

Think on the concept of throwing a ball as high as you can in the air. Eventually it will come down, that is what gravity does. He is simply trying to describe things he has never seen or known before. This also was the first war that introduced airplane warfare, attacks from the air was a new strategy. If you have ever seen an actual old war clipping, the bullets from these barrels can look like hail.

Revelation 8:8-9 *"The SECOND angel sounded his Trumpet, something like a huge mountain, all ablaze was thrown into the sea. A third of the sea turned to blood, a third of sea creatures died, and a third of the ships were destroyed."*

Some believe that the second Trumpet sounded during WWII. The atomic bomb that was dropped on Hiroshima and Nagasaki Japan in the summer of 1945 seems to display this mountain like fire, which also must have originated on Earth (John did not say it was a star or an asteroid or something from the sky). It was something *like* a mountain and mountains come from the earth, not from outer space. Both of these bombs combined killed over 100,000 people. I could see how the sea turned to blood. Also Japan from above looks small and is surrounded by bodies of water. Or it could have simply been the testing site of the first Atomic bomb in the desert or ocean.

There were a known 105,127 ships that participated during WWII (1939-1945), 36,387 of them were destroyed (an estimate of a third). Due to human error we may never know the exact sum of the ships involved, but this figure is still pretty amazing. Remember John is writing about 20th century stuff in the 1st century. So we need to see it through his eyes as he tries to explain what he is seeing. It would make sense that an atomic bomb explosion caused a big mountain, a blazing like a ball of fire. So this trumpet could have very well been blown during WWII. Again a third can refer to a time period or an area.

This six year war killed over 52 million people, which makes it the deadliest and bloodiest of all the wars to date. Prior to the twentieth century, no war in history has ever come close to a million dead. For the record even the Korean War, in a short three years (1950-1953) resulted in five million dead. Adding just these three wars together, totaling 13 years of bloodshed, with over 65 million dead.

Revelation 8:10-11 *The THIRD angel sounded his Trumpet, a great star, blazing like a torch, fell from the sky on a third of the rivers and springs. The name of the star is "Wormwood." A third of the water turned bitter and many people died from the water, because of its bitterness.*

Some believe that the third Trumpet sounded in 1986. Chernobyl is a Russian word for "wormwood." In April 1986 in Pripyat, Ukraine was the largest nuclear plant explosion the world had experienced. The Chernobyl nuclear disaster poured out ten times more radiation than both bombs dropped on Japan during WWII. A torch like contaminate radiation, fell from the sky from this disaster, after blowing upwards over a mile. The winds spread these toxic pollutants as far away as Germany, Sweden, Italy, and Great Britain. The waters around these areas a third became bitter. Cancer deaths reached over 125,000 with two million infected with 137 cesium's type radiation. Life expectance became 30 years, the land and surrounding area became ghost towns. The land was contaminated for 100s of miles. This region no longer can produce vegetation or livestock or quality of life. Cancer increased to 248% of the normal. This torch is something that is very hot, thousands of degrees. Nuclear radiation has the ability to melt or burn the skin off of human bodies. This in its self can symbolize a falling star, being bright red (hot). This one-third covers the area mass which has been infected.

The falling hail, fire, mountain, and star depicted here shows God's judgment on the physical world; earth, sea, fresh water, land, and stars. There will be a massive destruction of creation—a severe warning to a sinful people.

> **Revelation 8:12-13** *The FOURTH angel sounded his Trumpet, a third of the sun was struck, a third of the moon, and a third of the stars, so that a third of them turned dark. A third of the day was without light, and also a third of the night. I heard an eagle that was flying call out in a loud voice: "Woe! Woe! Woe to the inhabitants of the earth, because of the trumpet blasts about to be sounded by the other three angels!"*

Frequent use of thirds shows the destruction of creation will be catastrophic, and is also limited by God. Some sort of atmospheric condition or global pollution will reduce visibility or the sun's potency by a third – Eagle, some say can symbolize God's Wrath (or continued warning or judgment ahead), the "Woes" refers to announcements that the final three trumpets are going to get much worst. The first four trumpets affected the physical world, these next three will hurt mankind directly. Befalling on the inhabitant of the earth, describing those that are not followers of Christ and whom judgment will come upon.

Some believe that the fourth Trumpet sounded in 1989. The numbers of days shorten or the length of each day shortened. There would be a conflict with numbered days according with **Daniel 12:11.** He says, from the time the daily sacrifice is abolished and the abomination that causes desolation is set up, there will be 1,290 days. Some believe that this may have something to do with global warming, climate change or changed weather conditions. Jesus said, "Unless the days were [actually] shorten no one would survive" the "full" seven years or beyond this period (**Matthew 24:22** and **Mark 13:20**). So God can and has shortened the length of each day, it will and always will be seven years of total tribulation period or troubling times (the Days of Sorrow and Great Tribulation that covers the last three and a half years). So it's in keeping with God's prophecy, because God cannot lie and His word is true. And also because God is merciful He has lessened each day for us by one third.

Einstein's "Theory of Relativity," refers to time and speed as they are related to each other. So the hours in a day can and has been shorten or sped up. This relationship between Time and Speed means as one slows down so does the other, and visa versa. As much as this may not sound right or difficult to wrap your mind around, we are the ones that are limited in our own thinking or understanding. As for God nothing is impossible.

The birth of a new Globalization also began with the fall of the Berlin wall, in 1989. This may have started a new time clock. If the days were less and not shortened by human standard, the Bible would be a lie. Seven years is still going to be seven years, with God all things are possible. So the only logic to stand to reason is that the days have become lesser, with the time frame still intact. It seems difficult to understand how a third of our days have been shortened and we don't even realize it. This Trumpet is setting the stage for the signing of the Peace Treaty in the near future. Which former President Donald Trump's administration came very close to completing. No, he is not the antichrist! This Peace agreement will come through a third party, the antichrist with Israel's Prime Minister and Palestine's Hamas will sign it. Past presidents have failed to accomplish this task at Camp David.

Revelation 9:1-11 *"The FIFTH angel sounded his Trumpet, (1ˢᵗ WOE) a star has fallen from the sky to the earth. The star was given the key to the shaft of the abyss. He opened the abyss, smoke rose from it like a gigantic furnace. The sun and sky was darkened by the smoke. Out of the smoke locusts came down upon the earth. They were given power like scorpions on the earth. They were told not to harm the grass, plants, or trees; but only those people who did not have the Seal of God on their foreheads. They were not given the power to kill them, but to torment them for five months. The agony they suffered was like a sting of a scorpion when it struck. Men will seek death, but will not find it they will long to die but it will elude them. The locusts looked like horses ready for battle. Their heads wore something like a crown of gold, their faces resembled human faces. Their hair was like a woman's hair and teeth like a lion. Breastplates like iron and wings sound like thundering of many horses and chariots rushing to battle. Their tail had power to sting and torture for five months. A king over them the angel of the abyss whose name in Hebrews is "Abaddon" (destroyer) in Greek is "Apollyon" (destruction)."*

This angel, or possibly Satan because of the reference of a "fallen star" **Isaiah 14:12**, or one of his agents; God has given the keys to permit this terrifying event. In John's days the bottomless pit, the abyss meant dwelling place of the dead or demons. These locusts as well as frogs and flies were a part of the ten plagues God poured out on Egypt's ten main gods (**Exodus 7-11**). Locusts like all insects feed only on plants or on dead carcasses They are known to devour and destroy massive land areas quickly. Now they are told to not even touch them but to attack only mankind that is not sealed by God. These same locusts are given power as a scorpion. Just like beasts, birds, dogs, snakes, and scorpions; they all represent the same thing, "demonic spirits" (**Luke 10:19, I Corinthians 15:32**, and **Philippians 3:2**). Just like sheep we are also known as or like green trees planted by water; **Psalm 1:1-3, Proverbs 11:30,** or **Matthew 3:10**; there are many other scriptures throughout the Bible.

When Jesus healed a blind man, he first saw through his "Spiritual eyes" in **Mark 8:23-25**. These evil spirits will only attack and torment those that are (not) "sealed" by God. They will represent a powerful force that will torture mankind who do not follow God. They wreaked utter devastation on crops and were unstoppable, these locusts will now only attack unbelievers, and their short lived life is five months. They will suffer and yet will not die. Abaddon may also refer to Satan.

Some believe that the fifth Trumpet might have sounded in the early 1990's. In the 1990-1991 Gulf war, Saddam Hussein invaded Kuwait for their oil rich land. Saddam in Arabic which means "Destroyer"; his mother named him that because of the difficulty and painful child birth that almost killed her. The invasion of Kuwait was short lived; it lasted less than a year. As they fled Saddam's forces set about 700 oil wells ablaze. Since John isn't familiar with oil wells and their affects, he is using first century terminology. The smoke from the fires blocked the sun and sky for about three months; there was darkness during the day. John never said that it would cover the whole earth. Nor did he say for how long the sun and sky would be darkened or whether or not it was permanent. It seemed more like a land mass area. Where there is smoke there is also fire. A furnace has fire for its heat source. This all is coming from under the ground, John refers to this as a bottomless pit.

When I first read about these monstrous descriptions of these insects, I was in awe. A lot of readers seem to think that these are actually some type of creature insect. I used to think that way too. The locusts don't seem to refer to some kind of actual insect or animal at all.

Several pastor friends I know said we need to use caution in order to determine what is to be taken literally versus what should be taken symbolically or figuratively, when reading or studying the scriptures. I do not believe these locusts are actual insects. When talking about the things of God, never try to put or keep God in a box. Many churches have in fact suffocated God out by programs and standards of routine or are too busy playing with the gifts instead of communicating with the Giver of those gifts. He doesn't even feel welcomed in some of these churches. The sad thing is that some of these churches do not even miss God. Now the opposite is also true as well, placing Him too far outside the box is not beneficial either. Do not let your mind wonder into crazy thinking (**2 Timothy 1:7**). God could have very well been a complicated God; but He chose to have a relationship with His creation and make thing simple instead.

These locusts did not come from the bottomless pit, they were flying above it, coming down upon the earth. They came out of or through the smoke, not the fire of this pit. Power came from both ends of these locusts, they grouped as if they had a battle plan, wings like thunder or rushing chariots sounds. It also has a steel metal solid body, teeth like a lion; yet a human face? Why mention a woman's hair, unless for some reason it stands out to John. Common sense tells me that it must be some kind of war machine. They also have an apparently short life span of only five months. We don't know what has happened to these locusts only that they just disappeared. Again what can John possibly be describing from a 1st century view point? He is still in heaven looking downward at these events taking place. The state of the art helicopters and airplanes can easily fit what is actually being seen in his vision. The weaponry used from these aircrafts can be fired from the front or back, the iron plated shells, the blades sound can be like many chariots for battle, plus the human faces seen through the cockpit windows, attacking the people not plants. All of the flying squadrons from the United States military have painted figures on them.

Hussein's military force did not want to fight and would rather die than to return to Iraq. Instead they became prisoners of war. They were starving and no match against such fire power. They had thrown down their guns and surrendered willingly. This was the easiest and of all the least resisted conflicts that I know of. It is very difficult for me to think that this could actually be an insect, with such a horrific description.

Revelation 9:13-21 *"The SIXTH angel sounded his Trumpet, (2ⁿᵈ WOE) Release the four angels who are bound at the great river Euphrates. They have been kept ready for this every hour, day, month, and year to kill a third of mankind. The number of these troops was two hundred million. Horses and riders are as;*

breastplates were fiery red, dark blue, and yellow as sulfur. Heads of these horses resemble a lion's head out of their mouth came fire, smoke & sulfur. A third of mankind was killed by the three plagues; fire, smoke, & sulfur that came out of their mouths. Power of the horses was in their mouths and in the tails. The tails was like a snakes, having heads which they can inflict injury (weaponries of war). The rest of mankind still did not repent of the works of their hands; did not stop worshipping demons and idols of gold, silver, bronze, stone, & wood. They did not repent of their murders, magic arts, sexual immorality, or their thefts."

Beyond the Euphrates River lays Israel's enemies, Babylon (Iraq) and Assyria. This picture stands for God allowing a huge, destructive army to set out. God raises them up to carry out His will thus the notion of these armies being fallen angels. Describing these plagues: fire, smoke, and sulfur, snakes, emphasizes how horribly evil these troops are. Beast, birds, scorpions, and snakes can also be referenced to again as evil demonic spirits; also frogs, flies, and dogs.

What comes out of a person's mouth, so is he. Out of the abundance of ones heart, you speak (you become or are) (**Matthew 12:34-37**). They may stand for revolting, ferocious, and powerful demonic forces. This may also stand for a literal army, symbolizing a brutal military power which has caused untold blood shed throughout the centuries—the ten devastating plagues did not soften Pharaoh's heart. Though God was the One that harden his heart, to show how mighty God is. Great suffering tends to intensify whatever is in a person's character. If one is not already God fearing and tender, suffering may make them more so. If a person mocks God and is rebellious, suffering may increase these qualities. In the ancient world black magic often involved drugs and casting spells on people. This would involve evil spiritual forces, opposed of God.

Some believe that the sixth Trumpet sounded in 2001; possibly starting WWIII. The Euphrates River region area houses 100 percent Muslims countries. The terrorist attack of September 11, 2001 on the World Trade Center may have started WWIII. Remembering that all three of these World Wars started off small before they increased to a full blown battle.

Shortly after the attack on the United States, then President George W. Bush stated that this attack started WWIII and that flight 93 was the first U.S. countermeasure against the enemy. Former CIA director James Woolsey and former House Speaker Newt Gingrich both referred to this attack as the beginning of WWIII as well.

This war will be much different than any other war fought, for two reasons. One we will not know who the enemies are because for the most part they wear every day clothes, similar to the Vietnam War. And two, there will be a slow and consistent advancements. This war will be long and hard to win if even winnable. I do not regard this as WWIII, only time will tell.

We now have military forces in parts of the Middle Eastern Countries; I honestly don't see us getting out of this war any time soon, even though then President Barrack Obama tried. President Donald Trump made improved advancement to the good, without airing his battle plans, which the media wanted. He ordered killing of a few of the high ranking terrorist leaders, that weakened this terrorist group. What President Joe Biden did as an exit plan in August 2021 was an irresponsible and huge failure on many different levels. All of the American lives that were lost, wounded, or scared was all for nothing. President Biden left a gaping hole for the terrorists to get sucked into, while taking our troops out. He also left many behind to fend for themselves. His plan at best was horribly wrong, these countries are now helpless and defenseless. This war may not be quite over.

This is where it gets tricky, a third of mankind refers to the world's population. To kill a third of mankind would amount to about 2.3 billion people. The only nation or group with this remote capacity to have such an army of 200,000,000 strong is China or the State of Islam. This does not mean that allied forces cannot group together to equal such a large army. We also cannot rule out the possibility of the UN and or both EU peacekeeping forces. The fiery red, dark blue, and yellow like sulfur can possibly be a kind of war craft from these different forces.

It is also now possible to dry up the Euphrates River. In recent years Turkey had to stop the flow for one month to make repairs to their dam, which is where the Euphrates River flows out from. This lowered the level greatly and stopped the flow.

When we look at the history of the wars and conflicts we have faced in our world. We can see a pattern. It seems anytime we do not give the victory, win, or give honor to God, the next war or conflict will not be so pretty. During and after WWII we gave glory to God for the victories and prayed through a lot of those battles. The Korean War was a stale mate that ended up splitting a country in half. We did not seek much of the will of God or the favor of God, or even to acknowledge Him. It only lasted about three years from 1950-53, with a death total close to five million civilians and soldiers. That is still a lot of causalities in a very short span of time.

Or could it be that after WWII things started changing? Some historians think that the 1947-8 Supreme Court cases of Separation of Church and State may have triggered or placed these events in motion; Everson vs Board of Education and McCullum vs Board of Education. This was totally Unconstitutional and took Thomas Jefferson's personal interactions out of content. The Bible was the very first and only book used when schooling began in the 1600's. We started to stop prayer in our schools in the early 1960's. Instead we continued pushing God further out through the following decades, finally legalizing abortions in 1973. God considers abortion an abomination, yet He is still merciful, the damage could have been a lot worst; yet we still did not repent.

Then came the Vietnam conflict and it was horrible. It lasted for fourteen long years (1959-1973). Even though the death tolls were very low, totaling just shy of 60,000 (including MIA's). The physically crippling wounds, amputations, PTSD, and other mental scares toppled WWII at 300 percent and even Korea at 70 percent. The disability count to these veterans totaled 104,578; which was more than the previous two conflicts. There is a rule of thumb that any war that you cannot win within five years you will never win. It starts to decrease your chances by ten percent for each year that it goes beyond the five year maximum. During the first Gulf War as easy as it was, we still did not thank, honor, and glorify God for the win. I believe it was a test from God, in which we failed... again.

We are becoming more and more arrogant, boastful, and prideful. Cold hearted.

This makes a person wonder if our hearts have been growing cold towards God. It is believed that something huge must and will occur when the Rapture happens. Possibly a distraction to draw their attention from this event. Some think it would be alien abductions, POW, MIA or some other form of unaccountability. Or the possibility of some kind of special technological weapon capable of incinerating individuals. Most folks will only be concerned about themselves anyway, caring even less for their own families. As our hearts grow colder and colder, we start to care less and less.

Something to think about, of all the time frames in world history, at what point was it the bloodiest and what was the possible cause? If you said the last one hundred years, you would be correct. In all of humanity, the lost or wounded (or some other effects) total well over two hundred million deaths and causalities. This does not include the billions of dollars in reconstruction damages. The major cause was pushing God out and allowing Satan in.

> The angel and the Scroll **Revelation 10:1-4** *"I saw another mighty angel coming down from heaven. He was robed in a cloud, with a rainbow above his head; his face was like the sun, and his legs were like fiery pillars. He was holding a little scroll, which lay open in his hand. He planted his right foot on the sea and his left foot on the land, and gave a loud shout like a roar of a lion. When he shouted, the voices of the seven thunders spoke. And when the seven thunders spoke, I was about to write; but I heard a voice from heaven say, "Seal up what the seven thunders have said and do not write it down."*

Some scholars believe that this mighty angel is Jesus Christ. Other scholars believe that this angel is just one of the many Archangels in the Kingdom of God. Both Daniel and John have referred to Christ as the Son of Man or Lord in their visions. John described and identified who Jesus was at the beginning of Revelation and then later towards the ending. No doubt this angel is very powerful and has a huge stature. The Greeks translate thunder to mean a roar of authority. Again we have the number seven which is the spiritual completion or perfection number. John also wrote about another group of sevens at the beginning of **Revelation**; seven churches (**1:4-5**), seven spirits (**3-1**), seven lamps and spirits (**4:5**), and seven horns, eyes, & spirits (**5:6**). The thunderous (voice) are often referred to as God's judgment (also see **I Samuel 2:10** and **II Samuel 22:14**). These voices are unidentified, some believe that they are the voices of God. There was also another voice from heaven that told John not to write what the seven thunderous voices spoke of. We will never know what was said, it was for John's ears only. This interaction is placed between the six and seventh Trumpet, soon God's Wrath of judgment will commence on a sinful mankind. This angel has great or complete authority (equaling seven thunders).

> **Revelation 10:5-7** *"The angel I had seen standing on the sea and on the land raised his right hand to heaven. And swore by him who lives forever and ever, who created the heavens and all that is in them, the earth and all that is in it, and the sea and all that is in it, and said, "There will be no more delay! But in the days when the seventh angel is about to sound his trumpet, the mystery of God will be accomplished, just as he announced to his servants the prophets."*

There is no more delaying the final judgment and the actual Wrath of God to come very soon. He has given mankind every opportunity to repent the choices we have made and are now final. We are now also without any excuses. Once the Seventh Trumpet is blown it will usher in the Seven Vials of God's Wrath. This mystery usually refers to God's overall plans of redemption towards the human race. Earlier in the book of Revelation, God had a set total amount of people that were to be redeemed, by the use of His servants and messengers; prophets. The mystery of God has come to pass and is now accomplished.

> **Revelation 10:8-11** *"The voice that I had heard from heaven spoke to me once more: 'Go, take the scroll that lies open in the hand of the angel who is standing on the sea and on the land.' I went to the angel and asked him to give me the little scroll. He said to me, 'Take it and eat it. it will turn your stomach sour, but in your*

mouth it will be as sweet as honey.' I took the little scroll from the angel's hand and ate it. It tasted as sweet as honey in my mouth, but when I had eaten it, my stomach turned sour. Then I was told, 'You must prophesy again about many peoples, nations, languages and kings.'"

Some believe that this scroll could be the same as the one that had the seven Seals on it, that Jesus broke. This seems doubtful. Eating the scroll usually symbolizes understanding and accepting the message and to carry it out or to complete the mission. The message has two parts to it; the sweet side representing the Good News, Gospel, and Salvation to those that accepts and receives it. The other side being sour; representing the Condemnation, Judgment, and Wrath to those that refuse and denies the message. This is a picture of how followers of Jesus Christ are "only" the messengers and witnesses. We tend to take it out of content and beat people with our Bibles. We cannot make or force people to get Saved, that is the Holy Spirit's responsibility and job to convict them. Speak the Gospel truths and let the Holy Spirit do His part. There are also too many bad examples, we need to start showing the good side of Christ. John was finally told that he must prophesy to the whole world. This statement refers to us. At the time of the writing of Revelation, John was up there in age, he was well over 90 years old.

The Two Witnesses:

Revelation 11:1-6 *"I was given a reel like a measuring rod and was told, 'Go and measure the temple of God and the altar, and count the worshipers there. But exclude the outer court; do not measure it, because it has been given to the Gentiles. They will trample on the holy city for 42 months. And I will give power to My two witnesses, and they will prophesy for 1260 days, clothed in sackcloth. These are the two olive trees and the two lampstands that stand before the Lord of the earth. If anyone tries to harm them, fire comes from their mouths and devours their enemies. This is how anyone who wants to harm them must die. These men have power to shut up the sky so that it* *will not rain during the time they are prophesying; and they have power to turn the waters into blood and to strike the earth with every kind of plague as often as they want.'"*

It is believed that the two witnesses will be located at the Wailing Wall in the city of Jerusalem, at the Temple site. The Temple of God is also known as Solomon's Temple. It was first built in 957 BCE by king David's son Solomon. It was later destroyed by the Babylonians in 586 BCE. The Israelites were allowed to rebuild the temple a second time by a decree from king Cyrus in 536 BCE **(II Chronicles 36:23, also of Ezra)**. There are some supporting documents outside of the Bible that believe it was king Darius, but I have discarded this because it really does not matter at this point which king authorized it. I would rather believe the Bible than some outside source. The temple was later destroyed a second time by the Romans in 70 A.D.

The original temple had three parts to it; the outer court for the common folks, the inner court known as the Holy court for the priestly duties, and the Holy of Holies court strictly for the high priest once a year. It took about forty years or so to build the temple.

When the approval is given to rebuild the temple a third time all that would be needed is the (Holy place) altar for the sacrifices and the Holy of Holies. It will only take them a matter of a couple months to build, if that. They already have everything prefabricated and safely guarded to quickly build the temple when the time comes. John was only told to measure the important parts of the temple. The Israelites are the only worshipers that John had to count, the rest were given to the Gentiles to trample on for three and a half years. Some believe that the Gentiles are considered unbelievers or heathens, while some scholars simply say it refers to non-Jews.

The two witnesses are from a Jewish line, olive branch and lamp-stand would refer to Israel's linage. The Bible does not tell us where or how these two witnesses came to being, only that they just appeared. The Bible holds that an individual needs two witnesses to establish a true legal testimony **(Deuteronomy 19:15** and **John 8:17)**. The Bible does not clearly say who they are though some have speculated the two as one of the following: Enoch, Moses, Elijah, Elisha, or Isaiah. I believe they could be Enoch and Elijah, since they were the only ones taken up to heaven without a physical death. Or one of them being Moses which represents the Old Testament Law. They will be filled with boldness and authority in speaking the Word of God and will have supernatural powers for three and a half years. They cannot be harmed until their appointed time.

> **Revelation 11:7-10** *"When they have finished their testimony, the beast that comes up from the Abyss will attack them, and overpower and kill them. Their bodies will lie in the street of the great city, which is figuratively called Sodom and Egypt, where also their Lord was crucified. For three and a half days men from every people, tribe, language, and nation will gaze on their bodies and refuse them burial. The inhabitants of the earth will gloat over them and will celebrate by sending each other gifts, because these two prophets had tormented those who live on the earth."*

For three and a half years these two witnesses have now completed their convicting testimony to the whole world. The world has gotten so bad that no one wants to hear the truths. They have become nothing but cold, callous, evil people. If you think it is bad now, the worst is yet to come. The antichrist is now able to remove this annoying thorn from his side to lay hold of them and kill them. This could be where or when the antichrist becomes the hero of the world, getting rid of these trouble makers.

The people in the city did not even think to remove their dead bodies let alone bury them; they just laid there in the street for the whole world to look at. Or maybe the inhabitants might have thought the two witnesses had some type of disease and did not want to touch them or simply the hearts of mankind has grown cold and callous. Speaking the truths to a sinful mankind, in the hope for change is challenging or at the least difficult. They would rather stay in their selfish sinful nature.

Humanity seems to be a thing of the past. This great city represents the perverted wickedness of Sodom, the oppressiveness and bondage of Egypt, and of the rejected and crucified Christ of Jerusalem all rolled up into one.

Everyone started partying on, giving gifts, and having a good ole time joking and gloating over these witnesses. This would be a good place in time to crown the antichrist as the ruler of the world. The witnesses' true testimony tormented everyone that heard them speaking only goes to show that good and evil cannot and will not mix or cohabitate.

> **Revelation 11:11-14** *"After three and a half days a breath of life from God entered them, and they stood on their feet, and terror struck those who saw them. Then they heard a loud voice from heaven saying to them, 'Come up here.' And they went up to heaven in a cloud, while their enemies looked on. At that very hour there was a severe earthquake and a tenth of the city collapsed. Seven thousand people were killed in the earthquake, and the survivors were terrified and gave glory to the God of heaven. The second woe has passed; the third woe is coming."*

For three and a half days they just laid there on the spot for the entire world to see. Similar to the Garden of Eden (**Genesis 2:7**), God breathed the breath of life into the two witnesses. The inhabitants saw them wake up from the dead, stood on their feet and they heard the voice of God command them to return to heaven. As quickly as they came, they quickly departed riding into heaven on a cloud. The inhabitants could not believe what they saw and heard, they seem to be frozen in time shocked and horrified as this played out.

With technology today the entire world became the witness to these two men via satellite and internet. At that very moment a massive earthquake hits and destroys a part of the city killing and wounding thousands of people. This is the first time in the book of Revelation that evil people acknowledge God. So, saying they gave glory to the God of Heaven may not mean they had true repentance, it may only mean in their extreme terror they acknowledged a powerful God. They may be attempting to try to feed off of God's mercy, because they don't want to fall under the same type of judgment. God is no fool.

The two witnesses arrive for three and a half years and are given special authority and power not to be harmed until their time is up. Antichrist was finally allowed to kill them only after their time is up, they lay dead for three and a half days, all the world saw and witnessed this, through television and other electronic devices. The inhabitants celebrated over the death of these witnesses, they seem to be a thorn in their sides. After three and a half days they were raised, terror struck those who saw this. At that every hour there was a severe earthquake and a tenth of the city collapsed. Seven thousand people were killed the survivors were terrified and gave glory to the God of Heaven. Just going through the motions, but lacked true repentance.

This is the first time in the book of Revelation that evil people acknowledge God. So, saying they gave glory to the God of Heaven may not mean they had true repentance, it may only mean in their extreme terror they acknowledged a powerful God. Or simply they were looking towards the Heavens and not necessarily focused on God.

For the last hundred years Satan has been in full force more than ever before, knowing his time is extremely short. He has been able to cause a wedge or separation between God and His very own creation.

The removal of God in the school system started in 1947 via the supreme court decision, with Hugo Black as the deciding Supreme Court Justice. This was done by the twisting of the "Separation of Church and State" clause. It wasn't until 1964 that it was fully acted upon, by one atheist named Madelyn Murray O'Hara to remove prayer from our schools. Since the 1960's through 2015 there were 248 shootings in our schools with 982 dead and wounded. With each decade it slowly increased, in a matter of just six short years from 2010-2015, there were 109 shootings with 259 killed or injured. In another six years, from 2016-2021 there has been a total of 171 incidents with 115 deaths and 283 injured. Is school education really worth your child's life? Now would be a good time to homeschool your children!

> **Revelation 11:15-18** *"The SEVENTH angel sounded his Trumpet (3rd WOE), the loud voices in heaven said, 'The kingdom of the world has become the kingdom of the Lord and of Christ that will reign forever and ever.' The twenty-four elders said, 'We give thanks to you, Lord God almighty, the One who is and who was, because you have taken your great power and have begun to reign. The nations*

were angry; your WRATH has come. The time has come for judging the dead and for rewarding your servants the prophets and your saints and those who reverence your name, both small and great and for destroying those who destroy the earth."'

This is the "third time" the word **Wrath** shows up, after the Seals and the final Trumpet. This Wrath came out of the twenty-four elders' mouth, not God's. The Wrath of God is very close. The last Trumpet has sounded the Rapture has finally come, just prior to God's Wrath upon the whole earth. In this verse we can see that the Rapture is finally very close. There is more of a celebration from a sinful and suffering human kingdom, rather than a joyful and peaceful risen Christ Kingdom.

Many people are under the impression or subconsciously in their minds think and believe that the Seals, Trumpets, and the Vials are all crammed and happens during the short seven year duration. There is no evidence in scripture to support or back this idea up. The birth pangs in scripture does support the effects known through the Seals and the Trumpets, commonly known as the "Signs" of the times or the "Signs" of the End drawing near. Or of a final and pending Judgment.

Let's discuss the three differences:

SIGNS: they are things that can cause one to go in the right direction, like a road map or GPS. Or also to cause someone to think about something before they make a choice, such as danger or caution signs, or red light, green light. Or an outside influence, such as an alarm systems, security, or law enforcements; to make one to think of the repercussions of one's own choice's whether good or bad.

JUDGMENTS: they are punishments or corrections for bad behavior when one is caught, as within a legal system. This would not require a death sentence or major penalties, but yet payment of a fine, restitution, probation, or even a little jail time. A correction for bad behavior to give one a chance to repent.

WRATHS: they have been given every chance to conform, but refuse. They won't change their hearts, minds, or attitudes and have become a danger to society. They seem to put the blame on others, rather than themselves. As a last resort imminent eternal death for their unbelief. Mercy and grace have worn out and are no more.

Through the many different weapons of warfare from the last century, as seen through these Trumpets, we still continue to improve on how to kill and torture human beings. Now would be a good time to share with you a special kind of bomb we will also be facing. It is called an "Electric Magnetic Pulse" (EMP) bomb. This bomb, when detonated will fry everything including all electrical and electronic machinery, equipment and devices within its boundaries. This will include all types of factories, transportations, communications, satellites and power grids within its reach. In short, there will be no food, computers, phones, lights, gas, cars, A/C, or heating. Nada zilch nothing! This would literally take a nation back into a more primitive time period. It would cause survival wars within that country, such as looting as seen during the Covid pandemic in 2020-21. It would cause a country to become completely defenseless, creating wars within families among neighborhoods and businesses. Doing things that seem right in one's own eyes, such as defunding the police so that evil can abound even more. At this point Russia has such a weapon.

But I would be more concerned about the Country of China. They have been infiltrating the United States for the last few decades, with the assistance of multi-millionaires and billionaires under the guides of selfishness and greed (love of money & position); selling out our Country. These individuals are from Silicon Valley, Athletic Professional sports, Hollywood elites and several crooked and Corrupted Politicians. China also owns some property within our boarders. They are also responsible for the illegal drug problems coming in from our southern boarder which has originated from China. Oh, and they to also have the EMP Bomb capability.

These "three Woes" seems to be intensifying God's warnings. In addition to everything that is going on during these times, the last three Trumpets of Woes may show other signs as well. Can these three Woes be the same three described in Isaiah?

> *Woe to them that call evil good, and good evil; that put darkness for light, and light for darkness; that put bitter for sweet, and sweet for bitter!* *Woe to them that are wise in their own eyes, and prudent in their own sight!* *Woe to them that are mighty to drink wine, and men of strength to mingle strong drink; which justify (acquit) the wicked for rewards (bribes), and take away the righteousness of the righteous from them* (**Isaiah 5:20-23**)!

At this point what has been going on in the world around us? Going back to the year 1900 to the present, how does the school violence measure up per decades not counting the wounded, just in the United States:

1900 to 1909 = 35	1910 to 1919 = 19
1920 to 1929 = 55	1930 to 1939 = 21
1940 to 1949 = 21	1950 to 1959 = 27
1960 to 1969 = 104	1970 to 1979 = 63
1980 to 1989 = 181	1990 to 1999 = 193
2000 to 2009 = 182	2010 to 2019 = 338

Could this just simply be the effects of our nation removing God from our society? How far does a nation have to keep going to take God out before it is enough? Next we can look at how Mother Nature (major disasters, thousands of deaths or injuries and millions of dollars in damages) has measured up during the same time frame just in the United States alone:

volcano eruption = one
avalanches = three
wild/fire storms = fourteen
tsunamis = five
* derecho = two
blizzards = eight
heat waves/droughts/dust storms = seven
earthquakes = nine
floods = eighteen
multiple tornado outbreaks = twenty
tropical cyclones/hurricanes = fifty-two
* a widespread, long-lived wind storm that is associated with a
band of rapidly moving showers or thunderstorms.

Other major disasters, crimes against humanity (does not
include school shootings):

mass suicide attacks and arsons = six
military strikes (action) and State terrorism = four
bio/terrorism = six
mass murders = ten.

Most of these signs have been increasing within the last fifty years.
The evidence has always been there, only if one were to be looking
for them. All of this information is solely based on the United States
geographical area, and not the rest of the world. The birth pains are
there. We have been too busy doing life and have failed to see the Signs
happening around us. These are clear Signs, I am not making this
stuff up. It is time to wake up the church!

> **Revelations 11:19** *"Then God's temple in heaven was opened, and
> within his temple was seen the Ark of his covenant. And there came
> flashes of lightning, rumblings, peals of thunder, an earthquake
> and a great hailstorm."*

This is a repeat verse after the last Seal was broken (**Revelation
8:5**). It shows how organized God truly is. It makes sense for the Seals

and the Trumpets to stop at the same time. Where there is a beginning, a starting point there must be a stopping, finishing point. Just because the Seals are broken and the Trumpets are blown, does not mean they have stopped. Like labor pains, they will and do continue until the birth is completed or until the End.

CHAPTER FOUR

THE FAMOUS ALLEGORY

CHAPTER 12 OF Revelations: Some believe that this chapter in part deals with past, present and future events. The allegory of the woman and the dragon. I believe there is more to the beginning of this chapter. Such as a sign from the heavens (**Genesis 1:14**). There will be signs from the sun, moon, and stars.

> **Revelations 12:1-6:** *"A great and wondrous sign appeared in heaven: a woman clothed with the sun, with the moon under her feet and a crown of twelve stars on her head. She was pregnant and cried out in pain as she was about to give birth. Then another sign appeared in heaven: an enormous red dragon with seven heads and ten horns and seven crowns on his heads. His tail swept a third of the stars out of the sky and flung them to the earth. The dragon stood in front of the woman who was about to give birth, so that he might devour her child the moment it was born. She gave birth to a son, a male child, who will rule all the nations with an iron scepter. And her child was snatched up to God and to his throne. The woman fled into the desert to a place prepared for her by God, where she might be taken care of for 1,260 days."*

The woman is the nation of Israel, God's special people as shown by her clothing of the sun and the moon at her feet. The crown on her head is of a royal priesthood or kingship set apart unto God, the twelve stars represents the twelve tribes that make up Israel. The dragon represents Satan, the color red represents the pure evil and sinful nature, just like white stands for purity. Satan has been around since before the world was formed. The devil has always attacked anyone that God has blessed or favored, throughout the past, present and future. He has and will never change his hatred towards humanity. Satan hates humanity simply because we are created in <u>God's own image</u>. So he hates God, Satan is not capable of loving anyone or anything but himself.

The woman (Israel) gave birth to a son; Jesus Christ, His kingdom will have no end. God had protected Him during His earthly ministry. Once Jesus completed His sacrificial duties, He then took His rightful position seated on His throne and will rule the nations with an iron scepter. The seven heads of the dragon are believed to also be from the prophet **Daniel chapter 7: 4-7**, which includes; a lion, a bear, a leopard with four heads, and the beast. These animals are not separated like they were in the book of Daniel, they have become one big monster in John's vision. Each of these heads are different kingdoms or national governing countries, which Satan has been playing a part in. Or has at least influenced these nations. The ten horns are ten kings or political leaders. The seven crowns indicates that at one point these seven kingdoms (heads) were worldly power ruling kingdoms. The number seven in the Bible represents perfection or completion. This will be a complete and perfect evil monster.

The number ten in the Bible represents a divine testing or trial. There is coming a time very soon that our faith will be tested or will go on trial.

The third of the stars flung to the earth is believed by most scholars to be the original fallen angels that sided with Lucifer (**Ezekiel 28** and **Isaiah 14**). This is quite possible. They were not allowed in the third heaven which is God's throne room because of their rebellion, but now they are no longer welcomed in the second heaven either. (There are three heavens: the first is known as atmospheric heaven—which surrounds the earth and extends about a hundred or so miles above to the stratosphere, **Genesis 6:7** and **James 5:18.** The second celestial heaven refers to outer space or stellar heaven; sun, moon and stars, **Deuteronomy 4:14** and **Matthew 24:29.** The third heaven of heavens: spheres beyond which is visible from earth, God's Throne,

Deuteronomy 10:14 and **Psalm 148:4**. In all of these heavens, there are not anything more or less that makes up our universe.

In the near future the Jewish people will flee to a desert place where God has prepared and will protect them for three and a half years (1260 days), most theologians say this might be the Jewish nation returning to the promise land (of Israel). This stands to reason the Israelites fleeing from Judea to a secret place under God's protection. Other theologians do believe that Israel will have to go into hiding from the evil coming into the world, because it is going to get very bad. And at the same time God will be protecting them. This will happen at the second half of the seven year signed peace agreement as all hell breaks loose.

> **Revelations 12:7-9** *"And there was war in heaven. Michael and his angels fought against the dragon, and the dragon and his angels fought back. But he was not strong enough, and they lost their place in heaven. The great dragon was hurled down—that ancient serpent called the devil and Satan, who leads the whole world astray. He was hurled to the earth, and his angels with him."*

This battle has been going on since before the beginning of creation, Satan's uprising and quick fall from the third heaven, before the foundation of the world. Since Lucifer has already been kicked out of the third heaven, this conflict has continued in the first and second heavens. Now, very soon (if not already) this great dragon will be thrown out of the second heaven, along with the rest of his angelic army, which only leaves the first heaven... earth.

> *"From the days of John the Baptist until now, the kingdom of heaven has been forcefully advancing, and forceful men lay hold of it* (**Matthew 11:12**)."

In the spiritual realm there have always been a lot of activities between good and evil. When Jesus spoke these words, He was referring to the past and the present, the days gone by and the now or current days. In the spiritual realm there have always been a lot of activities, between good and evil.

During Daniel's twenty-one day fast in chapter 10, he was told by the Archangel Gabriel that he would have gotten there a lot sooner but was prevented while battling with the prince of Persia until the Archangel Michael came to help him (**Daniel 10:12-13**). The important thing to remember is to stay focus and stay the course. Your prayers may seem to get delayed but they are still on the way and at the right time. It may not make any sense to you now, but they will always be on time. This means we as followers of Christ cannot stay mushy or weak forever, it takes courageous dedication, bold and aggressive obedience. It is through these waiting periods that makes or breaks us. Remember that "All" things work out for our good (**Romans 8:28**). Stay diligent during life's race. Satan has been leading this world astray, it's all part of his plan. If you think things are bad now; it will get worse. Brace for shock!

> **Revelation 12:10-12** *"I heard a voice in heaven say: 'Now have come the salvation and the power and the kingdom of our God, and the authority of his Christ. For the accuser of our brothers, who accuses them before our God day and night, has been hurled down. They overcame him by the blood of the lamb and by the word of their testimony; they did not love their lives so much as to shrink from death. Therefore rejoice, you heavens and you who dwell in them! But woe to the earth and the sea, because the devil has gone down to you! He is filled with fury, because he knows that his time is short.'"*

Once the riff-raff is cleaned out from both second and third heavens, salvation and the power of God's kingdom with all authority in Christ draws ever so close. The banquet hall for the wedding feast is now cleaned up and all is being prepared. You can't have a party with a bunch of hoodlums and bandits hanging around. So, at this point Satan is no longer the accuser of the believers, day and night, since he has been cast out and no longer allowed or welcomed in the courtroom in heaven. He and his cohorts must be gone in order for the believers celebration to begin.

So many church folks believe that the Rapture happened way back in chapter four, simply because they claim the church is not mention anymore. This thinking is totally false. We (the church) have overcome Lucifer by the shed, sacrificial blood of Jesus Christ and by "our own testimony" of what He did when He saved us and became our King and Lord. This is not referring to the Israelites because most of them do not yet accept Jesus Christ as the Messiah and therefore would not have a need for a testimony as they are still living under the Law. But those that have accepted Jesus Christ as their Messiah have become the church and can witness their testimony. Jesus said, "and on this rock I will build My church and the gates of hell (Hades) will not overcome it" (**Matthew 16:18b**). These Saints of God did not regard their own life, but gladly laid it down. They became martyrs, not fearing death as they were persecuted through the ages.

From the first century to the present Christians have been martyred, more is yet to come. There is rejoicing in the upper heavenly places, because Satan is no longer allowed on the property. But dread to the inhabitants of the earth because the devil is filled with fury, anger and his (not God's) wrath, he also knows that he has a very limited time. The Tribulation and the Great Tribulation is not God's Wrath. From this passage it is Satan's wrath that came down to the earth filled with fury, not God's. The Wrath of God is swift and quick; it does not, nor will not last for seven or even three and a half years.

The main reason I believe that the Rapture happens after the last Trumpet is because the Bible does actually say "at the last trumpet or a sound of a trumpet" (**I Corinthians 15:52** & **I Thessalonians 4:16**). But mainly because it meshes and fits. The Rapture is not going to happen just for the sake of happening. We have made it sound more like some glorified resurrection of the living and the dead and simply watered down the true meaning of the Rapture. Remember the church is the "Bride." The banquet will be a private setting reserved only for the Bride and Groom, which follows immediately after the Rapture. Are you planning to wear stained, worn out, and torn clothing? Or are you planning to shave and bathe and look your best? Even though, according to **Philippians 3:21**, we will all be transformed into our own glorious bodies. This might only refer to our outward being. The Holy Spirit in the meantime has been working on our inside as we allow Him to. Being a true follower of

Jesus Christ has dwindled from the cost of carrying our cross "daily" (**Luke 9:23**). This can be something totally different.

We the churches need an overhaul to remove the corrupt sinful nature and hunger back towards Godliness. The way I see it we the church are not ready for the Rapture, many might be left behind. We need to stop faking it and lying to ourselves, and start getting real and share the same type of compassion for others that Jesus had when He was on this earth. Also be cautious and care like Jesus, because people will try to abuse and manipulate you. Be gentle as a Dove and wise as a Serpent (**Matthew 10:16**).

In the book of Ester, she went through six months of purification and another six months of cleansing before she was allowed to marry the king. A few theologians believe that the book of Ester is a real living allegory full of symbolisms and that this same thing can also apply to the church. This will cause a "falling away" or a rebellious revolt, **II Thessalonians 2:3**. We need to understand that the Rapture is a very huge deal and not some haphazard turn of events in God's time line. God will be cleaning up His Church of *all* unrighteousness and every unclean thought and sin. There will be no secret or entertaining, compromising sin that will not be dealt with. I do believe that the Rapture is just around the corner, but not until the purification and cleansing process are completed.

There is a gap between the Falling away in the church and when the Man of Sin is revealed. I believe it is within this gap that the Rapture happens. Remember not everyone that calls Jesus, Lord, Lord will enter heaven (**Matthew 7:21**). Even demons believe, and shudder (**James 2:19**).

Revelation 12:13-17 *"When the dragon saw that he had been hurled to the earth, he pursued the woman who had given birth to the male child. The woman was given the two wings of a great eagle, so that she might fly to the place prepared for her in the desert, where she would be taken care of for a time, times and half a time, out of the serpent's reach. Then from his mouth the serpent spewed water like a river, to overtake the woman and sweep her away with the torrent. But the earth helped the woman by opening its mouth and swallowing the river that the dragon had spewed out of*

*his mouth. Then the dragon was enraged at the woman and went
off to make war against the rest of her offspring—those who obey
God's commandments."*

Satan and his forces can no longer roam in the second heaven,
this battle has been going on long enough. God finally has His fill and
now it has come to an end. This can easily be a picture of how God is
making ready for the wedding feast, between the bride (the Church)
and the groom (Christ). The reception hall needs to be cleaned out
and put in order, for those that are invited to the feast. Satan and his
party of evil are not invited and have been evicted once and for all. The
devil has been persecuting the woman since God chose her and Satan
has put a bull's eye on them ever since. He has always tried to mess
up God's original plan, from the Garden until now.

The great eagle can be simply a large aircraft transporting the
Jewish people back safely to their promise land (Israel) or their secret
place. The eagle could also be a national emblem representing the
United States helping Israel. Some scholars believe this could describe
the United States helping and protecting Israel for two main reasons;
one, the United States has always supported Israel and two they have
always been their greatest allies.

Even though the Obama administration as well as many others,
such as Clinton, the Bush's, Carter, Ford, Nixon, and L.B Johnson (etc)
administrations had weakened this relationship some.

Now the current administration (Biden) has followed suit and
has not helped much if any. I am out to lunch on the whole "Build
Back Better" platform. I just do not see it. I feel sad for him, he is
not fit or strong enough for this office. I see a lot of shadowy figures
calling the shots and Biden is just a puppet. He did not really win the
election, it was stolen from Trump.

The "Puppet Masters" feared Trump that much. I will bless
though who bless you and curse though who curse you (**Genesis
12:3**).

Now the last thing I ever want is for any one person in the office
of the Presidency, to fail. When they succeed a country does well.
The Trump administration has greatly increased and improved the

relationship between the two countries. It just seems that the United States and Israel keep going back and forth in their relationship.

The other reason is that our national emblem just so happens to be the Bald Eagle (and Uncle Sam). Either way God uses this great eagle, showing that His hands will take care of them for three and a half years.

The water out of the mouth of this serpent is not actually water, it is referred to as a sea or multiple of people. The raging of many nations—they rage like the raging sea! Oh, the uproar of the peoples—they roar like the roaring of great waters! It is the many words that come out of our mouths. The Bible says that out of the abundance of the heart the mouth speaks (**Matthew 12:34** and **Luke 6:45**). This only shows how corrupted the world will become as they follow after these evil ways and thoughts. Although the people roar like the roar of surging waters, when He rebukes them they flee far away… (**Isaiah 17:12-13**).

God will divinely intervene to protect the nation of Israel from the armies of the world. The woman will not be overtaken, no weapon formed against them will prosper (**Isaiah 54:17**). A great earthquake will swallow up these enemies through Divine protection. God also did this in **Numbers chapter 16** to those that rebelled against His servant Moses, He can and will do it again. Lucifer has been so angry and has wanted to destroy Israel ever since the beginning. But now, he has been attacking her offspring, the adopted (Gentiles) Children of God, the Church. It is the "True" Church that is obeying God's commandments. It was never referring to the Jewish nation because they denied the Messiah.

In general, it is all about the Covenant of Grace, the New Testament believers. It was never about keeping the Old Testament Laws, they were impossible to obey and we could not keep them. It was too perfect and only showed that we needed a Savior. So it would not make sense to refer to the Old Testament Laws. It did serve its purpose and showed their sinful nature, which it only applied to the Jewish nation, not the Gentiles. From the beginning all God ever wanted was a relationship between Creator and His creation.

CHAPTER FIVE

BETWEEN THE LINES

Revelation 13:1-8 *"I saw a beast coming out of the sea that has ten horns and seven heads, with ten crowns on his horns, and on each head a blasphemous name. The beast I saw resembled a leopard, but had feet like those of a bear and a mouth like that of a lion. The dragon gave the beast his power and his throne and great authority. One of the heads of the beast seemed to have had a fatal wound, but the fatal wound had been healed. The whole world was astonished and followed the beast. Men worshiped the dragon because he had given authority to the beast, and they also worshiped the beast and asked, 'Who is like the beast? Who can make war against him? The beast was given a mouth to utter proud words and blasphemies and to exercise his authority for forty-two months. He opened his mouth to blaspheme God, and to slander His name and His dwelling place and those who live in heaven. He was given power to make war against the saints and to conquer them. And he was given authority over every tribe, people, language and nation. All inhabitants of the earth will worship the beast all whose names have not been written in the book of life belonging to the Lamb that was slain from the creation of the world.'"*

THIS LOOKS TO be the same animal in chapter twelve without the harlot sitting on this beast, which represents gross wicked sinfulness. We are now given more details here. This has now become one monster

94

of a beast, the One World Government system (kingdom). From the time of the first century until now, all throughout history the Saints of God have been martyred by individual countries and powers. Now it seems that the whole world will be against them with no safe place to go. It is no longer separated (like in **Daniel chapter 7**) they all became united as one. Daniel gave a more personal description of the fourth beast in the vision, **verse 7** as terrifying and frightening and very powerful. It had large iron teeth and bronze claws, it crushed and devoured its victims and trampled on whatever was left.

It looks as if each past kingdoms has formed together to finally become one. These animals are kingdoms that have become one, joining together with the beast. The ten horns are ten kings that will rule the ten territorial regions. The ten regions are broken down as: 1) North America, Canada and Mexico (NAFTA); 2) European Union countries (EU); 3) Japan [These first three regions are considered the Trilateral Commission and are the main representatives that are running the world's monetary system. They are also possibly the three horns in **Daniel 7:8** that were or will be uprooted by the little horn, antichrist. The first three must be taken out or down in order for the One World Government to happen.] 4) Australia, New Zealand and South Africa; 5) Eastern Europe, Pakistan, Afghanistan, Russia and former Soviet Union countries; 6) South and Central America, Cuba and the Caribbean Islands; 7) Middle East and North Africa; 8) Central Africa; 9) India, South and Southeast Asia; and 10) China (includes Mongolia).

It was the same (mentioned earlier) Bilderberg group that released a report in September 1973 forming these ten regions written above. As it stands this document regionalized an adoptive model for a Global One World System.

More details were given in Daniel chapter seven; the first animal was a Lion with wings of an Eagle which were torn off. The wings were lifted from the ground and stood on two feet like a man and was given a heart (or mind) to it. Some scholars say that the following are Great Britain as the Lion which is their national emblem. The torn off Eagle's wing could display a forced separation of independence from Great Britain creating the United States. Both the Eagle as well as a man (Uncle Sam) heart (**Daniel 7:4**) are known emblem of the United States.

The second animal was a Bear, the national emblem of Russia. A strong and powerful animal having three ribs between its teeth, it is told to get up and eat its fill of flesh (**Daniel 7:5**). The ribs can symbolize three different legal systems, smaller governments, or nations. Russia will attack three and afterwards devours much flesh.

The third animal was that of a Leopard with four heads and four wings of a bird (Fowl) on its back. A lot of folks want to believe that these four heads are the four generals from Greece, during and after Alexander the Great's rule. If that was the case this animal would not be in John's vision, the leopard would have been a past prophecy. So in theory it would not fit and does not make any sense for God to refer to the ten toes and ten horns as kings and then jump to a full scale head to represent the same thing. The whole of each head from this animal are considered by most as being likely the rise and fall of the same nation or country. What makes more sense is the country whose national emblem also just so happens to be the Leopard is Germany, which has risen and fallen three times. Lastly the Fowl or Rooster which is the national emblem of France (which also came out from Germany).

The final note here is that God is a very purposeful and detailed God. He does not waste any part of any visions or dream. The wings of the fowl and the eagle and the man with a heart are significant. If it was important enough for God to include them in this dream, we would do well not to ignore them. While a lot of folks choose to overlook them they are still very important to understand. When it came to the interpretation, Daniel was only told about the four beasts and he never asked about the rest of his dream,

> **Daniel 7:16-28:** *"I approached one of those standing there and asked him the true meaning of all this. So he told me and gave me the interpretation of these things. The four great beasts are four kingdoms that will rise from the earth. But the saints of the Most High will receive the kingdom and will possess it forever—yes, forever and ever. Then I wanted to know <u>the true meaning of the fourth beast</u>, which was <u>different from all the others</u> and most <u>terrifying</u>, with its <u>iron and bronze claws</u>—the <u>beast that crushed</u>*

and <u>devoured its victims</u> and <u>trampled underfoot</u> whatever was left. I also wanted to know about the <u>ten horns</u> on its head and about the other <u>horn that came up</u>, before which <u>three of them fell</u>—the <u>horn that looked more imposing than the others</u> and that had eyes and a mouth that spoke boastfully. As I watched, this horn was <u>waging war against the saints</u> and <u>defeating them</u>, 'until the Ancient of Days came and pronounced judgment in favor of the saints of the Most High, and the time came when they possessed the kingdom.' He gave me this explanation: The fourth beast is a <u>fourth kingdom (the eight in overall total) that will appear on earth. It will be different from all the other kingdoms and will devour the whole earth, trampling it down and crushing it.</u> The ten horns are ten kings who will come from this kingdom. After them another king will arise, different from the earlier ones; he will subdue three kings. He will <u>speak against the Most High</u> and <u>oppress his saints</u> and <u>try to change the set times and the laws.</u> The <u>saints will be handed over to him for (three and a half years)</u> a time, times and half a time. But the court of God will sit, and <u>his power will be taken away</u> and <u>completely destroyed forever.</u> Then the sovereignty, power and greatness of the kingdoms under the whole heaven will be handed over to the saints, the people of the Most High. His kingdom will be an everlasting kingdom, and all rulers will worship and obey him. This is the end of the matter. I, Daniel, was deeply troubled by my thoughts, and my face turned pale, but I kept the matter to myself."
I think he was simply horrified and didn't think to ask.

The national emblem for Germany is the Leopard, the four heads refer to the possible rise and fall of Germany; known as Reich, which in English is translated as realm or empire. The first Reich was the holy Roman empire from 800-1806 (fell), the second Reich German empire known as the Ottoman empire from 1871-1918 (fell) and the third Reich the greater German empire from 1933-1945 (fell) during WWII. At this moment Germany is gaining momentum in authority and power.

The fatal wound, some believe was the Berlin wall separating democracy and communism. This wall lasted from 1961 to 1989 (**Daniel 7:6**). While others believe it to be an actual person, this does not seem likely, since there has never been any human being on the planet to cause or move the whole world to mourn or to respond all in the same way or manner.

The Fowl represents France's national emblem and the relationship between the two countries. When Germany was eventually downsized France was formed. There was also a German-Franco alliance. They fought together during World War II, as well. There are crowns on each of these horns and on each of the heads were blasphemous names. This time each of the horns is the ones that had crowns on them, unlike the previous chapter where the heads were crowned. This is possibly where the ten world regions started forming as some believe. The beast resembled a leopard (Germany), it had feet like a bear (Russia), and a mouth (English language) of a lion (Great Britain). The dragon (Satan) gave the beast (the one world's governing system) power, his throne, and great authority. The one that will be in charge of the beast system will be the antichrist. One of the heads of the beast (kingdom) had a fatal wound which was healed (the Berlin Wall). Now again any fatal blow to any one person just does not seem possible to astonish the whole world. Not one person in our historical past has ever been able to astonish the "whole" world. Nope not one! Mother Teresa, Princess Diana, Elvis, Michael Jackson, JFK, MLK, RFK… not even Jesus Christ Himself. If this holds to be true in August of 1961 the Berlin wall has mortally wounded Germany, splitting her from east to west. In November of 1989 the wall was taken down, the wound was set to be healed. Both of these dates made big headlines throughout the media world.

Also for your information Satan cannot bring anything or anyone back to life. He has no power or ability to do so. He is only known as death and destruction (among other things). Only God is the giver of life, regardless of what Hollywood or others may say.

The bear being Russia's national emblem is as well a major communist country. The bear will be as strong as Russia and in their beliefs. The lion being Great Britain, this beast will speak English. The whole world will be astonished and follow after this beast (the world economic system) worshipping both beast and dragon, that was given authority. Who can make war against him? The beast's mouth uttered proud words and blasphemies and exercised his authority for forty-two months. The beast will be allowed to make war against the saints, a far cry from peace keeping. It seems that the saints of God have become more of a threat to the One World Government. The UN and EU will or may have (joined alliance) authority over every tribe, people, and nation. This may also include the World Health Organization (WHO) as well. For the saints of God it will be a win-win situation. Paul said, "For to me, to live is Christ, to die is gain (**Philippians 1:21**)." I also find it interesting that when the secular news media or magazines refer to these countries they also reference these animals.

The reason why some theologians believe that these animals represents different countries, is all about how God has always kept things in an orderly purposeful structured format. He has always wanted to be understood as the changes happened since borders and births of new nations are constantly rising and falling and splitting apart. These countries have not been known at the time of its writings. The New World was not known at the time. For example; Canada, Australia, North, South, and Central Americas. So God used what would describe each of these countries by their national emblems. They did not exist yet until their appointed time. During the time of **Ezekiel's** writings, **chapters 38** and **39** refer to kingdoms that exists then and has been renamed in our time, such as; Magog (Russia), Persia (Iran), Meshesh/Tubal (Former Soviet States), Gomer (Eastern Europe), Togarmiah (Turkey), Cush (Sudan/Ethiopia) and Put (Libya). Even though these countries will have their part in the End Times, their purpose will be different from the other countries that make up this beast. It would not make sense for a harmony, unity and orderly characteristic of God to use Magog instead of the bear; and then use the lion, eagle, fowl and leopard (which have not been established yet). In short God is simply not a messy haphazard kind of God! God truly is keeping it simple for us.

We must first understand that the statue image in **Daniel chapter two** are not the same kingdoms in **Daniel** vision in **chapter seven**. Well, at least not the first three kingdoms. The last kingdom of iron legs (Rome) has brought forth four other kingdoms, under a different country name. I will discuss this a little later in chapter seven.

There will be a total of eight kingdoms (this includes the beast's reign) from the time of Daniel and to the End of the Age, not just a total of four. The first set of four kingdoms refers to the immediate future that follows from Daniel's era. The fourth kingdom (Rome) branched out the next group of four which some believed to be for the distant future. God is not repeating Himself here, at the same time God is showing us that some of these kingdoms will reappear. This is because they all become a part of each of the last kingdom. Each past kingdom continues, in part, to linger into and affect the next kingdom's power.

Daniel has another vision in **chapter eight** about a "Ram and a Goat", this whole chapter refers to the coming End Times. In verses **19-26** of the same chapter it explains the meaning;

> *"I am going to tell you what will happen later in the time of WRATH, (the Days of Sorrow or of Great Tribulation) because the vision concerns the appointed Time of the End. The two-horned ram that you saw represents the kings of Media and Persia. The shaggy goat is the king of Greece, (these kingdoms will make a comeback) and the large horn between his eyes is the first king. The four horns that replaced the one that was broken off represent four kingdoms that will emerge from this nation but will not have the same power. In the latter parts of their reign, when rebels have become completely wicked, a stern faced king, a master of intrigue, will arise. He will become very strong, but not by his own power. He will cause astounding devastation and will succeed in whatever he does. He will destroy the mighty and the holy people. He will cause deceit to prosper, and he will consider himself superior. When they feel secure (the seven year contract), he will destroy many and take his stand against the Prince of princes (those in political power). Yet he will be destroyed, but "not by human power." The vision of the evenings and mornings is true, but seal up the vision, for it concerns the distant future.*

The dragon is Satan, the beast is a political governing system and these heads are kingdoms that will make up the system. The one that will have the overall authority and free reign is the figure of antichrist. The ten horns will be individual persons, kings or rulers in their designated empire region.

Revelation 13:11-18 *"There is a second beast. Having two horns like a lamb; but spoke like a dragon. He exercised all the authority of the first beast on his behalf, and made the earth and its inhabitants worship the first beast, whose fatal wound had been healed. And he performed great and miraculous signs, even causing fire to come down from heaven to earth in full view of men. Because of the signs he was given power to do on behalf of the first beast, he deceived the inhabitants of the earth. He ordered them to set up an image in honor of the beast who was wounded by the sword and yet lived. He was given power to give breath to the image of the first beast, so that it could speak and cause all who refused to worship the image to be killed. He also forced everyone, small and great, rich and poor, free and slave, to receive a mark on his right hand or on his forehead, so that no one could buy or sell unless he had the mark, which is the name of the beast or the number of his name. This calls for wisdom. If anyone has insight, let him calculate the number of the beast, for it is man's number. His number is 666."*

A false prophet, looks innocent as a lamb, but spoke evil. Also the horns in prophecies represents a king or a leader, though some say it could be a kingdom or a nation, and a lamb would represent a sacrifice atonement offering, a foreshadowing of Christ (Christianity based). So it would seem that two nations or leaders (horns) will come together under the guidelines of Christianity and or human-itarian motives. This can easily fit the United States that came out of England (during the 1400's-1600's religious reform and religious freedom). The lamb would represent a nation with religious beliefs or ties, during the crusader era and the State (government) run churches. During this time oppression and persecution period birthed two countries (the horns), Great Britain and the New World America. Or some say the horns can possibly refer to the United Nations and the European Union, but not likely. So it does not make sense that it would be an actual false prophet as a person, but a much bigger type of a religious system. Any regards to a beast in Bible prophecy by some is considered a type of kingdom or some form of a system. To keep it in simple form, it will be huge. A beast equals a monster!

This second beast will have just as much authority as the first beast. It will cause all the inhabitants to worship the first beast. This second beast did great miraculous signs, causing fire to come down from heaven mimicking the likeness of Elijah in the Old Testament (**I Kings 18:38**); which was one of many signs of magic that he would perform. Some believe that this beast might be given access to military fire power in order to cause this fire to come upon the earth. He will be able to deceive many. He will also order an image statue to be built in honor of the first beast that was healed from his fatal wound, possibly from Germany. Some say there will be two images built. One will be the first beast and the second one will be that which was wounded. But John does not mention two. He, the false prophet will cause the statue to speak and caused those that refused to worship this image to be killed. This can be high technology or some kind of magic for evil used. There have been reports of curses and or demons that can attach themselves to objects. We already have Artificial intelligence (AI) being used in homes, cars, and phones as ways to communicate back and forth with us. We are now at a point where we can speak to something, such as Alexa, and it will follow the command.

The Greek word that we use in English for image is actually "icon." Jesus used the same wording when He asked whose icon (not image) (**Matthew 22:20**) is on the Roman coin. The definition for icon is likeness, similar to or represents. Icons are used everywhere in our society; in computers, cell phones and currencies. They represent a value or likeness to a belief that is geared towards an understanding of something. So an icon or image may not necessarily be an exact portrait or statue of something or someone.

The one question I had was what or how would this image statue look. John does not give any details; just that it is in fact will be some kind or type of image statue being worshipped, with the ability to communicate and talk. We just assumed that it would take on some kind of human form. But both of these beasts are two types of a World System. Could it even be a Hologram or simply speaking back and forth into thin air?

In the 1830's came the first radio and telegraph, then the birth of the telephone came shortly afterwards in the 1870's. The boom of the entertainment business started in the early 20th century. In 1928 the television was birthed, going quickly from silent to audible, from black and white to color, and from a few channels to several hundreds of channels. This increased the speed of electronics and high technology spreading across the world, in a very short span of time; in less than 100 years. Though television started off with some Christian based morals, more than it is today, we hear and see more dysfunctional lifestyles of foul language, violence, nudity, sexual immorality, homosexual perversion and actions.

In 1936 began the birth of the computer age that would come with the endless internet access information highways and games galore in the years that followed (1980's +). Then came the satellite systems, not only can this technology send messages, transfer funds, transmit audio or video pictures and conversations, but also can pin point a dime from space. This in itself has the capabilities to track any individual anywhere on the planet. China spies on their own citizens using this technology.

In saying all this, do you think we have been deceived yet? John could not describe this beast, it is indescribable. It will come down to keeping us preoccupied from the things of God. I am not saying that all this technology is evil or is all bad. But I am saying give to God what is due to Him, you. See things for what they are. There is some good without compromising your integrity. There are endless things that can take time away from us. God really does not mind that we have technology. He's the one that gave it to us in the first place. It is what we do with the knowledge and information that matters. It has become more and more out of balance and has been spiraling out of control. God never wanted to be number one or first place in your life, but He does desire to be in the center of it. Think about it, if Satan can keep you from thinking, knowing, growing, worshipping or communicating with God, don't you think he would do it. Keeping us weak is his specialty; My people perish for the lack of knowledge (**Hosea 4:6**). His job is to keep you from God, in the dark. So, whether you believe Satan exists or not, it does not make a difference. In any given twenty-four hour period, how much of it do you spend with God? Ask your children, the ones with their faces in their cell phones and iPads for hours at a time. My grandchildren would have a fit if it was taken away from them. It has become their life support, instead of God. I understand that life happens, but God still needs and must be the top priority in our life.

Joshua 1:8, says, *"Do not let this Book of the law depart from your mouth, meditate on it day and night, so that you may be careful to do everything written in it. Then you will be prosperous and be successful."*

In addition to all this, Satan also has been using the government to attack and make the church even weaker. Yes, we are "legally" being attack through unlawful laws to silence us. In essence telling us to sit down and shut up. The churches used to have a big impact in the affairs (direction) of the country (government). Most political figures had a stance in Biblical morality. This all started to change little by little at the turn of the twentieth century.

The times have changed since I grew up. We never had a computer and we all turned out fine. The family only had one box television if you were lucky, maybe two. Which were mainly in black & white, some channels were in color, with only a few channels. If you worked the knob good enough you might get more channels. Oh, and we also had to physically get up to change the channels, oh the pain of it all. Now it's normal to have three to five or more flat screen TV's, one for each room in the house. It has become the center of our lives, our furniture is now being dictated by the television's location.

We also had one phone that had to stay connected to a power source along with its cord (the leash that prevented you from walking the yard for privacy). We had the original family shared minute plan, you would only get ten minutes at one time and I was clock watching for my turn. We also only had one car and it seemed to work out well. I remember walking or riding a bike everywhere I went, and sometimes it was five miles away. Oh how I must have suffered the pain of it all. I never once demanded or bugged my parents for what I was able to do independently on my own. I get that things are nicer and more convenient but we over step them when we replace them for God. We have gotten too lazy with all these technological stuff. This new normal is extremely dangerous. How far are you willing to go to keep pushing God out, to say enough is enough, I need you GOD.

So many Christians don't understand the seriousness of keeping and maintaining their personal relationship with God real. They don't study, pray or even open and read their Bibles, except maybe on Sundays. And they still think of themselves as Christians. The shameful thing is we don't even need to open our Bibles in some churches. We now have the conveniences of a big screen that shows and illustrates scriptures for us. We are in danger of weakening our Christian walk. They can spend hours feeding on worshipping this beast, yet not even spending any time with God. The influences have weight down many that have turned away from God. And those that do give time to God are considered evangelical religious extremist. You cannot have both the world and God. You must choose "one" whom you will serve (**Matthew 6:24**). Many folks are at the mercy of this beast and they don't even realize it yet.

This beast will try to control our every thoughts if we let him or give into him. The power of suggestion and the hidden sins weaken the Christian's desires to then entertain different thoughts away from God. We are in an era where hypnotic states and tapping into the subconscious minds are very possible through our senses. Mainly, but not limited through our hearing and seeing. Great care needs to be taken at what might be using up our time or the attention we give it. As in the hours we spent on the computer, watching television or gaming activity in a given 24 hour period. Do not allow the present state of our world's way of thinking to become your "new" norm.

In the mid 1930's there was another game changer. We started programs like Social Security, Welfare, Food Stamps, and other public assistance. It may have started out with good intentions and for *temporary* relief. The more children one had the more dollars one received. More and more people seemed to stay on them, thinking they could not do any better or out of plain laziness or selfishness.

Boredom can cause one to do crazy things, having excess time on your hands can cause problems. The government also makes it difficult for these individuals to try to help themselves and to get on their feet. As soon as they try to do better for themselves and their families, to become more productive in society the government removes these services too quickly. Then they end up falling right back on their faces. They need to be able to wean themselves off of them. So they become stuck in a rut with nowhere else to go.

The government also prefers individuals to depend upon them for their needs. The government has made it too easy and comfortable for the struggling poor. Ben Franklin saw this same problem in the late 1700's in England. This government gave assistance to the poor allowing them to be comfortable in the state that they were in. Franklin said, this is wrong they will never change or want to do better for themselves, it is necessary to cause them to be uncomfortable in their present state. It was not to shame them, but to challenge them to make themselves better.

In an interview in 2008 on Fox news several folks voted for their Presidential candidate, all because he was promising them free stuff. Placing anything above or before God is called idol worship. I foresee this coming to an end very soon, since we are a broke country. Whatever happened to hate what God hates and love what God loves (**Romans 12**). Again we can read in **Proverbs chapter four**;

> *"Listen, my sons, to a father's instruction, pay attention and gain understanding. I give you sound learning, so do not forsake my teaching... Lay hold of my words with all your heart, keep my commands and you will live... do not forget my words or swerve from them... I guide you in the way of wisdom and lead you along straight paths... hold on to instruction, do not let it go; guard it well, for it is your life... My son, pay attention to what I say, listen closely to my words. Do not let them out of your sight, keep them within your heart, for they are life to those who find them and health to a man's whole body. Above all else, guard your heart, for it is the wellspring of life. Put away perversity from your mouth; keep corrupt talk far from your lips. Let your eyes look straight ahead... keep your foot from evil."*

We have never really gotten out from under the Stock Market crash of 1929 and the Great Depression of the 1930's. It has been a glooming shadow for almost a century. It has been covered up with all of the governmental programs that have been sustaining our economy. Our country's present unemployment rate is at about 8-10 percent. When the programs crumble, and they will, unemployment will spike to around 24 percent. Even though the current administration seems to have lowered the unemployment rate down to about 3-4 percent. Some believe it may go even higher than that. All it did was put a bandage on the problem, the problem was never fixed, the wound has been continuously bleeding. Again it was suppose to be temporary until one got on their feet, never permanent. We have slowly but surely been preoccupied and been conforming to the ways of this world. Control a people, control the country. Paul warned us in **Romans 12:2**,

> *"Do not conform any longer to the pattern of this world, but be transformed by the renewing of the mind. Then you will be able to test and approve what God's will is, His good, pleasing and perfect will."*

The false prophet will have authority over this second beast system and will seem to be the driving force for the antichrist. He started to force everyone to receive a mark on their right hand or forehead. No one will be able to buy or sell without this Mark. This Mark is the name and number of the first beast; 666. This is the number of man, not of a man. We are told to call for wisdom in order to understand and be able to calculate the number of this beast. This tells me that someone will have the insight to figure out the truth behind the motives. And be able to identify who is behind them.

The original Greek wording for 666 is "chi xi stigma". Thayer's Greek dictionary defines Stigma which comes from a primary root word "stizy." to stick, to prick. A mark incised or punched for recognition of ownership. This marking can easily go under the skin such as a microchip, more than likely. Some say possibly a tattoo or a surface marking, to display ownership similar to past slavery markings. But this does not seem to be the case.

The barcode numbering system has three sixes in them, as guards or guide bars; at the start, the middle and the ending. From the starting point to the middle are called classifiers describing the product's name and the type. From the middle to the end of this section are the identifiers, such as location, country, factory or company where the product came from (individual information).

Also China and India are the first countries that came out with an individual chip with a person's complete medical history. These implants are being used on pets and new born babies in parts of the world. The Radio Frequency Identification (RFID) cards are the new and improved ID cards for the very near future. This invention will not only just be able to isolate a person per country, but can also be used internationally. This will include tracking (GPS) your every moves, plus if you're a fugitive or terrorist (according to their standards), they will find you. This would include what you buy or don't buy. The technology in just the last century has by far surpassed anything we've seen throughout history.

I do not believe that this would be considered the actual "Mark" of the beast. The Mark in question will require one to have to make a choice, our alliance or denial to either the government or to God and Christ. This will be a choice that one will need to make as to whether or not one receives this Mark. You will have to make a clear cut and dry choice to flatly denounce God and hold a complete alliance to the beast (Satan). There will be no mistake you will know exactly what you are doing. A stand for or against, all in or all out, black or white there will be no gray areas. You will know what you are doing, there will be no playing dumb. I believe we might be Raptured out prior to this stage but this is only a guess. We will be forced to make a choice—without it we will not be able to buy, sell, eat, or work.

Revelation 14:1-5 *"I looked and before me was the Lamb standing on Mount Zion with Him the 144,000; that had His name and His Father's name on their foreheads. I heard a sound like (symphony) harpists playing; they sang a new song before the throne and the elders. No one can (learn or have the ability to) sing this song, only the 144,000 who had been redeemed (rescued) from the earth."*

They kept themselves pure and did not defile themselves sexually or immorally, nor did they conform to the world's standards; they followed the lamb's lead. They were purchased among men and offered as First fruits (set apart) to God and the Lamb. They were totally blameless and without spot. These 144,000 were rescued and set apart for a purpose from among humanity during this time period. Possibly martyred tribulation saints for Jesus Christ, as a witness to the entire world. Can offering and sacrifice mean the same thing? They gave of themselves as living sacrifices. Most theologians believe that they are also the same 144,000 from the twelve tribes mentioned earlier. Given the tribe of Dan's historical past, it stands to reason why they were excluded.

> **Revelation 14:6-11** *"The three angels- the first angel in midair had the Eternal Gospel, proclaim to the whole earth in a loud voice, 'Fear God and give Him glory, the hour of His judgment has come. Worship Him alone as creator of all things.' The second angel followed, saying, 'Fallen is Babylon the great city, has made all the nations drink the maddening (wrath) wine of her fornication' (adulteries). The third angel followed, saying loudly, 'if anyone worships the beast or his image, receiving his mark. The same shall drink the wine of the WRATH of God, which is poured out undiluted into God's anger. They will face the torment of fire and agony of sulfurous flames before the holy angels and the Lamb. The smoke of their torment will rise throughout the ages for eternity. Day and night will come and go without pause or cessation (no rest). There will be no end to the torture experienced by those who worship the beast and his image, by those that received the mark of his name.'"*

Burning sulfur and the torments are commonly associated with hell. This describes the unending suffering that will await all those that has given their allegiance to worldly evil, doom to those who will submit to the beast. They are condemned to experience God's full anger eternally. The Christians, no matter what the cost, are to remain faithful and true.

The first angel proclaims the never ending Gospel throughout the whole earth, a holy fear to God, praise and honor to Him, the moment of His Wrath has arrived. God alone is to be worshiped as our Father and Creator of all things. The second angel speaks about the great city of Babylon is destroyed, the sin capital of the world. This may be the place where the Cups (not Seals or Trumpets) of God's WRATH will start from and spread over the whole earth. The third angel follows with the effects to come to those that received the Mark, absolutely no rest or peace forever. The agony and torture will continue throughout all eternity, we will be able to see their punishment.

God has clearly given us examples in the Bible on what it means to fall under His Wrath. Such examples could be the Flood of the planet during Noah's day, or the destruction in the valley of the five kings (Sodom and Gomorrah) during Abraham's time. And at other times, all to destroy the evil once the cup of Wrath was full and over flowing and He was still able to protect and cover the righteous.

> **Revelation 14:12-13** *"A call for patience and endurance on part of the saints, that keeps His commandments and are (stay) faithful to Jesus. A voice heard out of heaven saying, 'Blessed are the dead who die from now on (or until the end). Yes, they will rest from their labor, their deeds (works) will follow (remain with) them.'"*

Are these saints the same as the 144,000 mentioned in the seventh chapter, since possibly the church has been Raptured (or very soon), at this point? The days of sorrow of the second half of the tribulation is all that remains. Regardless, being elected means being set apart from or for something else, a purpose, duty, job or calling. Since the 144,000 are not mentioned, many believe the reference of faithful saints keeping of the commandments are the tribulation saints. I believe they will be the martyred saints during the tribulation period.

> **Revelation 14:14-20** *"I looked and one sitting on a white cloud like the Son of man, with a golden crown on His head, in His hand was a sharp sickle. Another angel came out of the temple, calling loudly to Him sitting on the cloud, 'Take Your sickle and reap, the time to reap has come, to harvest the earth for it is ripe.' He that was*

seated on the cloud swung His sickle over the earth, and the earth was harvested. Another angel came out of the temple in heaven, having also a sharp sickle. Still another angel, in charge of the fire, came from the altar, yelled out to the one with a sharp sickle, 'Take your sharp sickle and gather the clusters of grapes from the earth's vine, its grapes are ripe.' The angel swung his sickle on the earth, gathered its grapes and threw them into the great winepress of God's WRATH. They were trampled in the winepress outside the city, and blood flowed out of the press, rising as high as the horses bridle for a distance of 1600 stadia."

So when will this Rapture happen? There are four hints given in scripture:

1. Jesus taught that the rapture would occur immediately after the tribulation (**Matthew 24:29-31**).

2. Only when those killed during the tribulation are resurrected, the bible says, "This is the first resurrection" (**Revelation 20:4-6**).

3. Our gathering together unto Him cannot happen until after the antichrist is revealed (**2 Thessalonians 2:1-3**).

4. The rapture happens at the "Last Trumpet" when the kingdom of this world becomes the Kingdom of Our Lord and His Christ (**I Corinthians 15:24-28** and **Revelation 11:15-19**).

When everything is complete there will be two simultaneous harvests (**Matthew 13:24-30**). The wheat are the children of God and the tares are the children of the wicked one, the enemy is the devil, the harvest is the End of the World Age and the reapers are the Angels of God. In **Matthew 14: 14-16** refers to the (fruit or Saved) wheat harvest, while in **Matthew 14: 17-20** refers to (weeds or lost) tare harvest.

This is where the Rapture happens, not earlier as some are convinced. Furlongs or stadia are about 160-200 miles depending on what translation you use. North of Kidron Valley to Jerusalem is approximately 160 miles at Armageddon. The Son of Man refers to the Messiah, associated with Jesus Christ. The crown and sickle signifies that Christ is both King (Victor) and Judge(er). The New Testament harvest depict gathering of God's children. The first harvest means the saints will be *protected from God's Wrath,* which is released at the second harvest. The winepress relentlessly crushes grapes, symbolizes the force of God's Wrath to those that rebel against Him. The sickle is what is used by farmers during harvest time. Some believe since the Church has been Raptured at this point and that the Holy Spirit has been removed from the face of the earth as well.

There are two types of harvest here. Jesus spoke about this in His parable of the wheat and the weeds (tares) in **Matthew 13:24-43**. There will be a short time lapse between these two harvests. This will all happen after the Last Trumpet and before the Vials are poured upon the earth. The second harvest is said to be the great winepress of God's Wrath (the tares). Some theologians believe the winepress describes the great "Armageddon War". This can also be what the harlot and the nations that took the Mark of the Beast will be forced to drink.

> **Revelation 15:1-2** *"I saw in heaven another great and marvelous sign: seven angels with the seven last plagues because with them **God's WRATH** is completed. And I saw what looked like a sea of glass mix with fire and, standing beside the sea, those who had been victorious over the beast and his image and over the number of his name."*

God's Wrath is against those who reject Christ as Lord and Savior, and those who persecuted believers. God is righteously angry because He is just and thus will judge evil. Some think that these three sets of seven are all part of the Wrath of God; the Seals, the Trumpets, and the Bowls that were executed or started during the early years of the church. Other thinks they represent judgments during the times between Christ's first and second comings. Still others believe they are predictions of God's Wrath just prior to Christ's return, during the Seven Year count down in the Tribulation. I believe that the Seals were more of God's Signs of the Times and the Trumpets were more like God's Final Warnings or Judgments. God will always use correction first, before His Wrath. Lastly you cannot simply just pour out a Seal or a Trumpet, it would not make any sense. But you can pour out of a Vial or Bowl.

Though the beast initially persecutes and is thought of as conquering believers, his only short lived success is to eliminate those that stand firm in the Faith. Jesus Christ wins the final battle and guarantees the beast's defeat, through which believers are able to overcome this evil. For the true Christians there are no defeats, only victory. Because of God's love and merciful ways, He has always used warnings and corrections prior to His Wrath. His judgments are not necessarily His Wrath either, though they can be very painful but not destructive. On the other hand His Wrath will destroy a population, nation or world. His Wrath has always been as a last resource, He gains no pleasure in sending anyone to Hell. No true Christian will ever suffer any part of His final Wrath. Only when God has used all possible ways to change or convert one's thought or way of thinking, and the choices made are final, we will receive our rewards whether good or bad. . . (**Ecclesiastes 12:14**). God has always been a God of chances.

A lot is going on between the Seventh Trumpet in chapter 11:15 and through to chapter 14. The Seventh (last) Trumpet has sounded so we have finally been Raptured. At the same time frame from this Trumpet, there will be two witnesses that will show up. They will have power and will prophesy for three and a half years (1260 days). When their time is complete, the beast will be allowed to kill them. They will rise from the streets after three and a half days and ascend into heaven. Some believe this may signify the beginning to the last half of the Tribulation (Days of Sorrow), which would make sense. That they left just prior to Armageddon, shows that God has given every possible way for humanity to repent.

We have the allegory in chapter 12 that shows Lucifer's hatred towards God's chosen people and His adopted offspring, those that are followers of Christ. Satan has been warring with Israel a lot longer than he has with the Gentile Christians. In chapter 13 we have discussed the two types of (systems) beasts. One of them coming out of the sea, a multitude of people that represent the "One World Governmental system." The other beast is the one coming out of the Earth represents the "One World Religious system," which will mandate the Mark.

Just prior to the Rapture three angels were flying in midair. Some say this could possibly be the second Heaven. The first angel had the eternal true Gospel to proclaim to all the nations of the Earth. The second angel sounded that Babylon the Great that has caused the nations to drink the sexually perverted wine, of God's Wrath, has fallen. The third angel warned loudly those that worshipped and took the Mark of the beast, they will also suffer the fury of God's full Wrath and the cup of His anger, there will be no rest from it day or night. Right after all this the harvest of the Earth has finally come. We are Raptured from the Seven Vials that contains the fullness of God's Wrath.

> **Daniel 9:27**, *"He will confirm a covenant with many for one week, but in the middle of the week he will put a stop to sacrifice and offering. And the abomination of desolation will be on a wing of the temple until the decreed destruction is poured out on the desolator."*

John's Revelation does not mention this important information. The one full week or seven days will be a seven year signed contract between Israel and antichrist. He is very good at what he does, deceptions, lies, and manipulations of not just the world but also to God's very own elect. Antichrist will default on this agreement three and a half years later. At this half way point (1260 days) he will stop all the animal sacrifices. It is the Jewish customs to have the first sacrifice of a red heifer which is a vitally important process for cleansing and purification of the altar, only then will the animal sacrifices commence for the daily sacrifices (**Numbers 19**). What is interesting is the "red" heifers were thought to have been extinct; they have been found just a few decades ago. They are now heavily guarded and cared for even to this day. These red heifers are very important, without them the Jewish people would not be able to even commence their altar sacrifices, according to their tradition. The red heifer is the only thing that must be used to sanctify and purify the altar first, before even being able to start ceremonial sacrifice.

The Jewish people are still searching for the Messiah, they never accepted Jesus Christ as the last sacrificial Lamb. One other point is you cannot have an altar without a built Temple. This will be the third time the Temple will be rebuilt. It normally would take several years to complete. They have already prefabricated all the walls and are in storage, waiting for the go ahead. To finish the Temple will only take a matter of a few days or weeks, possibly months but not years. This only deals with the inner court, what is known as the Holy Place and the Holy of Holies, the outer court will belong to the Gentiles. Jesus referenced the abomination of desolation to this prophecy in **Matthew 24:15** and **Mark 13:14**. Antichrist will claim to be God and the long awaiting Messiah, and that there will no longer be a need for the offerings. He will order the destruction of the Temple for the last and final time.

The Muslim's are also looking for their own messiah. But unfortunately their messiah will closely resemble the characteristics of Antichrist. According to their belief he will cause wars, destructions, and persecutions, much like what is happening in our present lifetime.

CHAPTER SIX

THE VIALS, THE WRATH POURED

Revelation 16:1-4, 8-21 *"I heard a loud voice from the temple saying to the seven angels, "Go, and pour out the seven bowls of God's Wrath on the earth. The* **First** *angel went out and* **poured** *out his bowl on the land, and ugly and painful sores broke out on the people who had the mark of the beast and worshiped his image. The* **Second** *angel* **poured** *out his bowl on the sea, and it turned into blood like that of a dead man, and every living thing in the sea died. The* **Third** *angel* **poured** *out his bowl on the rivers and springs of water, and they became blood… The* **Fourth** *angel* **poured** *out his bowl on the sun, and the sun was given power to scorch people with fire. They were seared by the intense heat and they cursed the name of God, who had control over these plagues, but they refused to repent and glorify Him. The* **Fifth** *angel* **poured** *out his bowl on the throne of the beast, and his kingdom was plunged into darkness. Men gnawed their tongues in agony and cursed the God of heaven because of their pains and their sores, but they refused to repent of what they had done. The* **Sixth** *angel* **poured** *out his bowl on the great river Euphrates and its water dried up 'to prepare the way for the kings of the East.' Then I saw 'three evil spirits' that looked like frogs; 'they came out of the mouth of the dragon, out of the mouth of the beast and out of the mouth of the false prophet.' They are* **'spirits of demons performing miraculous signs,'** *and they go out to the kings of the whole world, to gather them* *for the battle <u>on the great day of God Almighty</u>. 'Behold, I come like a thief! Blessed is he who stays awake and keeps his clothes with him, so that he may not go naked and be shamefully exposed.' Then they gathered the kings together to the place that in Hebrew is called **Armageddon**. The **Seventh** angel **poured** out his bowl into the air, and out of the temple came a loud voice from the throne, saying, '**It is done**!' then there came <u>flashes of lightning, rumblings, peals of thunder and a severe earthquake</u>. No earthquake like it has ever occurred since man has been on earth, so tremendous was the quake. The great city splits into three parts, and the cities of the nations collapsed. God remembered Babylon the Great and gave her the cup filled with the wine of the fury of his wrath. Every island fled away and the mountains could not be found. From the sky huge hailstones of about a hundred pounds each fell on men. And <u>they cursed God on account of the plague of hail</u>, because the plague was so terrible."*

THESE SEVEN BOWLS are of *God's actual Wrath,* that are poured out one right after the other, in concessions without any rest, brake, gap of time, or a breather in between. The voice in heaven (God) said to GO and they finally *went;* the seven angels actual left heaven to initiate these bowls upon the earth. God's Wrath is always personal and hits directly to destroy His target, evil people. People will be shocked that the God of love has another side of Him called His justice, Wrath; His righteous anger. They still ignore and disobey God so much that some escalated even more towards their opposition by striking against those things that represent's God. Those that were left behind after the Rapture occurred. So there will be more and more bloodshed, attacks. The darkness can also symbolize a type of plague that occurred in Egypt, the Israelites still had light in their dwelling (**Exodus 10:21-23**). Or darkness at Christ's crucifixion (**Matthew 27:45**). Some theologians say that this could be God turning His back on the sinful evil on the planet. This can describe a kingdom in confusion and chaos. When there is a power outage there is a whole lot of looting.

The king from the Eastern location can be anyone in that direction from the nation of Israel, since to the western boarder of Israel has a water mass (the Mediterranean Sea). Most scholars believe this would be Iran, which has a pure hatred for His chosen nation. But it can still be anyone that surrounds them, including Russia, Syria, Sudan, Iraq and Libya or any combination.

The three evil spirits that came out of the dragon, the beast and the false prophet will be so strong, that it will still lead people deceived to follow their own evilness and selfish desires. Some believe that this is a counterfeit trinity; the dragon (god, Lucifer), the beast (antichrist), and false prophet (unholy spirit). The two things that may cause these kings to get involve to do battle, are their natural hatred or blindness towards God and the truth. Or some supernatural miraculous signs convincing them that they cannot possibly lose and siding with the beast.

During the seven bowls being poured out, mankind never showed any remorse or true repentance of its evil sinful ways. Instead they just showed more and more of their true colors by getting in God's face and at point blank, outright cursing God. God's actual Wrath is now poured out.

The meaning of God's Wrath is He has always delivered or sent (messengers) His angel(s) to perform this duty unlike the Seals or the Trumpets. Also God's Wrath has always been a pouring out of something. These angels went out in order to fulfill the pouring of God's final Wrath on earth. Another thing is that God's Wrath has never been slow, but quick and fast, one right after the other in order of completion, unlike the Seals and the Trumpets which are slower.

Once God has done everything possible for mankind to repent, His Wrath is paramount and comes to pass. So why would God even do such a thing, since His mercies are everlasting (**Psalm 100:5**; & **136:1**) and His grace is new every day (**Lamentation 3:22-23** & **II Corinthians 12:19**)? The answer can be found in **Zephaniah 3:5,**

> *"The Lord within her is righteous, He does no wrong. Morning by morning He dispenses His justice, and every new day He does not fail, yet the unrighteous know no shame."*

God has given them all the chance to turn from their wickedness, now their fate is sealed.

This is the third and final time that this verse (**16:18**) has been repeated. Each time it showed up after completing their sequence of events, from the last Seal, the last Trumpet, and now the last Vial. God is a unified, harmonious, and purposeful God.

> **Revelation 17:1-4** *"Come, I will show you the punishment of the great prostitute, who sits on many waters. With her the kings of the earth committed adultery and the inhabitants of the earth were intoxicated with the wine of her adulteries. Then the angel carried me away in the Spirit into a desert. There I saw a woman sitting on a scarlet beast that was covered with blasphemous names and had seven heads and ten horns. The woman was dressed in purple and scarlet, and was glittering with gold, precious stones and pearls. She held a golden cup in her hand, filled with abominable things and the filth of her adulteries."*

Many scholars say that the great prostitute will be linked to the New Babylon, she will symbolize all the different cultures that are unfaithful towards God. The prostitute and New Babylon are one and the same. The many waters are multitudes of people, nations and tongues that have been following or are ruled by the harlot. A centralized place of business that is well populated and traveled. Her drunkenness indicates celebrating and partying, and a carefree, decadent life style. The woman sitting on the beast can likely be the prostitute. She agrees with everything the beast represents. She is riding and sitting as if she is in charge. The scarlet color (reddish) of the beast represents everything impure and sinful, the total opposite of the color white for purity. In the book of **Isaiah 1:18,** alludes scarlet (red) to sins. This beast is so full of himself and its sinful ways that the beast's skin turned red. The woman in scarlet is just as abominating as the beast. Purple is also the color for royalty, she fancies herself with self-honor and being of high self-esteem position. As in kingly, having dominion, royalty, empire, authority and the ruler. The scarlet represents all the opposites of God. She is also wearing sparkling jewelry and fancy clothes. She is so into herself, so full of sin that she is seen here drinking more of her detestable things. She is surely addicted to herself and thinking she is above the law and God. This is actually explained in the next few verses.

> **Revelations 17:6-18** *"I saw that the woman was drunk with the blood of the saints, the blood of those who bore the testimony to Jesus. When I saw her, I was greatly astonished. Then the angel said to me: 'Why are you astonished? I will explain to you the mystery of the woman and of the beast she rides, which has the seven heads and ten horns. The beast, which you saw, <u>once was, now is not, and will come</u> up out of the abyss and go to his destruction. The inhabitants of the earth whose names have not been written in the book of life from the creation of the world will be astonished when they see the beast, because <u>he once was, now is not, and yet will come</u>. This calls for a mind with wisdom. The seven heads are seven hills on which the woman sits. They are also seven kings. Five have fallen, one is, the other has not yet come; but when he does come, he must remain for a little while. <u>The beast who once was, and now is not, is an eighth king</u>. <u>He belongs to the seven</u> and is going to his destruction. The ten horns you saw are the ten kings who have not yet received a kingdom, but who for one hour will receive authority as kings along with the beast. They have one purpose and will give their power and authority to the beast. They will make war against the Lamb, but the Lamb will overcome them because he is Lord of lords and King of kings and with him will be his called, chosen and faithful followers.' Then the angel said to me, 'The waters you saw, where the prostitute sits, are the peoples, multitudes, nations and languages. The beast and the ten horns you saw will hate the prostitute. They will bring her to ruin and leave her naked; they will eat her flesh and burn her with fire. For God has put it into their hearts to accomplish his purpose by agreeing to give the beast their power to rule, until God's words are fulfilled. The woman you saw is the great city that rules over the kings of the earth.'"*

The Angel has already explained what John was seeing. The woman drinking the blood of any kind would be a grim horror evoking the thoughts of cannibalism (See **Isaiah 34:5-6, 49:26** and **2 Kings 6:26-29**). She is so hungry for innocent blood that it is the only thing that satisfies her own desires and thirsts. The three stages some believe represents the beast's rise to power its wound and recovery, this is not from John's time frame but the perspective of prophesied events. Some say this has to do with the Berlin Wall falling, while others say this was at the end of WWII, and the British Empire which fell from power. The bigger picture may simply be Lucifer, that was once one of the archangel's in Heaven. Now he will come again to face God at his judgment doom (**Isaiah 14:12**). At any event this wound of recovery has nothing to do with an individual person. One view links these kings to Roman rulers, such as Augustus, Tiberius, Caligula, Claudia and Nero as the five that have fallen, with Vespasian as the one who is, and Titus as the one yet to come. This is totally false limiting these kings to one kingdom. We must look at this from a world view point. It would make more sense to conclude these as known empires, from John's time line. So there have been five fallen empires at the time of John's writings. The five that have fallen are Egypt, Assyria, Babylon, Media-Persia and Greece. The one that is, was the Roman Empire. The one to come was the British Empire. The eighth and final kingdom is yet to come: Globalization.

The seven hills are two folds, an actual place located in Rome and seven kings. This can possibly be where the headquarters will be during the final stage. Others believe these kings that have ruled their kingdoms from the past; Old Babylon, Assyria, New Babylon, Media- Persia and Graeco-Macedonia. And the present day as Rome; followed by the future nation of the antichrist. Yet this one does not account for the eighth kingdom, this only includes seven kingdoms. What about the eighth one? Animals in Bible prophecy always refer to kingdoms or nations, never as a king or an individual person. In Daniel chapter seven these same animals are individual kingdoms that were separated at the time. But now they have become one with the beast in Revelation, attached to as one massive leadership.

Small parts of an animal, such as horn, finger, or toes would refer to a single ruler, leader, or king. They now have a boss to answer to. Britain was the one to come as the seventh empire. The last and final empire will be coming soon. Not to confuse this with Daniel chapter two, regarding the statue vision king Nebuchadnezzar had. That starts off with kingdom one Babylon (gold), kingdom two Media-Persia (silver), kingdom three Greece (bronze), kingdom four Rome (iron) and the last kingdom five (mixed with clay and iron). Most scholars have concluded this as the revived Holy Roman Empire. This being the only exception, which was explained as present and future kingdom to come, it made up the fullness of this statue. The statue as a whole represents the earth and the associated different metals ruling kingdoms until the End of the Age. The stone that is thrown and crushes this image will be Jesus Christ's kingdom without an end. The ten toes of this statue and the ten horns have the same meaning as in ten kings ruling their divided regions.

The second theory was close; there is no need to count Babylon twice. What seems to make more sense are the fallen empires as Egypt, Assyria, Babylon, Media-Persia and Greece, which have all fallen during John's writing. Rome is in the presence, in John's day, and Britain as the seventh kingdom has not yet come. When he does come, he must remain for a little while, late middle-age. In our world history France, England and Britain have battled against each other. Britain has become Great Britain to this day, the new world power at that time. The eighth kingdom, many believe as the United Nations and or the European Union, the new and improved "Revived Holy Roman Empire" which was established in 2009.

There are over twenty different cities on our planet claiming to be built on seven hills. Many believe that it must be from the city of Rome, since the Bible says the antichrist will come from the Rome Empire. These are not the same areas. Now remember the Roman Empire covered a huge geographical area not just Italy. One more thing to think about, the U.N. has several countries in their membership from the Roman Empire. So it is very possible the antichrist can come out from the United Nations.

The beast has always been around since the beginning of time. It has been a part of every rise and fall of each kingdom, and has grown stronger with each era. As one falls, the beast just moves on to the next. They all had several things in common. They are all gentile, secular and heathen controlled empires in a nut shell, an army of evil genocides. They also carried with them many false gods, religious beliefs, rituals, and worship. There have always been wars, no peace only greed for power authority to rule the whole earth. They all hate and despise any Christian or Godly belief (or anyone of Jewish descent) that does not conform to theirs. They would be considered a threat to their evil way of thinking. A cold evil heart toward humanity comes to mind. This is the main conflict that will never allow any type of unity upon the earth.

None of these kingdoms were Christian based or sold out for God. On the contrary, it was always about putting a wedge between the creation and the Creator. Though the Israelites ruled their own kingdom in peace for a short time, they did not last every long, because they kept turning away from God and His Commandments. Yet at the same time they were not interested in trying to take over the world, like the others. God gave them their shared inheritance in the Promised Land not the promised earth.

In this scripture it also says that the beast belongs to the seven, this is the present tense. Even though the past kingdoms have fallen, the beast never did fall. It has become a part of them that did not fall. It seems that this beast has been carried over from kingdom to kingdom. In the end it finally faces its own destruction. In so doing this will combine together to become one last government, soon to come.

The beast and the prostitute are both wicked and greedy. They will be at odds with each other full of selfish hatred and thirsting for power. This conflict in the end destroys the prostitute. She is left naked. They that were eating her flesh could be the inhabitants or animals. I believe that they were her followers, because John would have said wild animals, if that were the case. God had His hand in this; He allowed the beast *their* authority and power to rule. The use of "their" makes it plural, referring to the Bear, Leopard, and Lion in addition to the singular beast.

I would like to now briefly cover again what Jesus said about these Endtime events. In **chapter ten of Matthew**, Jesus calls them together and gives them authority and power over evil spirits and all manner of diseases; and to preach (missionaries were born). In this chapter are some very powerful instructions for witnessing what we are to be doing, and also what to expect through persecution. None of His disciples had any major problems. If any of them did, it would have been recorded.

> **Vs. 16**, *Sent as sheep among wolves, be wise as serpents and harmless as doves.* **Vs. 17**, *Beware of men; they "will" deliver you to (town) councils and scourge (flog) you in their synagogues* (churches). **Vs. 18,** *You "will" be brought before governors and kings for My name sake (in a court of law), a testimony (witness) against them.* **Vs. 19**, *When they deliver you up (and they will), take no thought (be not anxious) what you shall say; it shall be given to you what you shall speak at that time.* **Vs. 20**, *It will not be from or come from you, but the Holy Spirit of your Father that will speak in (through) you.* **Vs. 21**, *Brother "shall" deliver up his brother to death, and the father his child; children "will" rise up against their parents, and cause them to be put to death (family divisions).* **Vs. 22**, *You "will" be hated by all men for My name sake (because of Me); he that endures (perseveres) to the "End" shall be saved.* **Vs. 23**, *"When" they persecute you in the city, flee into another; truly I say, you shall not have finished, until the Son of Man comes (returns/ second coming).* **Vs. 24-5**, *A disciple (student/servant) is not above his master (teacher or lord). It is enough for a disciple to be like his master and servant his lord. If they call the master or lord of the house Satan (or Beelzebub), how much more shall they call his household the same?* **Vs. 26-7**, *Do not fear them; there is nothing covered (concealed), that will not be revealed (disclosed); hidden, that will not be known. What I tell you in the dark(ness), speak it in the light (daytime); what I whisper in your ear, proclaim it upon the rooftops.* **Vs. 28**, *Do not fear them that can kill the body, but cannot kill the soul; rather fear Him who is able to destroy both body and soul in hell.* **Vs. 32-6**, *If you confess Me before men, I will confess you before My Father in heaven. If you deny Me before men, I will deny you before My Father in heaven. I came not to bring peace on earth, but a sword. I come to set a man in conflict against his father, daughter against her mother; in laws against in laws. A man's enemies will be the members of his own house (family).*

This prophecy began after Jesus Christ's ascension into heaven, from the first century to the present. None of this happened while Jesus was with His disciples.

In **Matthew chapter 24,** Jesus starts off, *take care (heed) that no man deceive you* **(Vs. 4)**. *Many will come in My name, claiming to be Christ, deceiving many* **(Vs. 5)**. *You will hear of wars and rumors of wars, do not be troubled by it, all these things must come to pass, but it is not yet the End* **(Vs. 6)**. *Nation will rise against nation, kingdom against kingdom; famines, pestilences, and earthquakes in various places. All these are the start (beginning) in sorrows (birth pains)* **(Vs.7-8)**. *You will be delivered up to be afflicted (tortured), and be killed, you will be hated of all nations because of Me (this includes your own country). Many shall be offended (abandon their faith, turned away) and shall betray and hate one another* **(Vs. 9-10)**. *Many false prophets shall (appear) come and go (rise) and shall deceive many. Because of their iniquity (lawlessness) that will abound (few will obey the laws); the love of many will become (grow) cold. There will be no end to the increase wickedness* **(Vs.11-2)**. *He that endures (don't waver from the path) to the end will be Saved. This gospel will be preached in all (throughout) the world as a witness to (testimony of) all the nations (and people), then shall the End come* **(Vs. 13-4)**. *When you see the (detestable thing) abomination of desolation (sac religious object), standing in the holy place* **(Daniel 11:31)**, this will be an actual person not a statue. *Those that are in Judea flee into the mountains* (**Vs. 15-6**).

Revelation's 8:5, 11:19, and **16:18** are identical and the same scripture verses. They all happen and are completed at the End of the Age. Though they all started at different time periods, there is not one single time line, such as:

[starting point→——**SEAL**s→——**TRUMPET**→——**VIAL**s→——ending point],

but there are three simultaneously time lines. They started at different time periods and continue up to the final and same ending.

The **SEAL**s—the longest periodicity-[→—possibly after John's writing→—until the end–]

The **TRUMPET**s—the next longest periodicity-[→—possibly start of 20th century→until the end–]

The **VIAL**s—shortest and quickest periodicity-[→—last couple years or months→until the end–]

They began or will begin at different times and will all end or stop at the same final EndTime. So the Seals will continue as the Trumpets starts and continues, as the Vials begins. Eventually all three will be in unison until the end. None of these will cease or stop until the End.

CHAPTER SEVEN

WHAT SAITH DANIEL

TO AVOID REPEATS I will only highlight briefly what I have already covered in this book. At the same time I will go through only the chapters dealing with what applies to End Time prophecy according to Daniel's writings of visions and dreams.

In **chapter two,** king Nebuchadnezzar statue dream is explained in verses 38-45. *"In your hands He (God) has placed mankind and the beasts of the field and the birds in the air. Wherever they live, He has made you ruler over them all. You are that head of gold. After you, another kingdom will rise, inferior to yours. Next, a third kingdom, one of bronze, will rule over the whole earth. Finally, there will be a fourth kingdom, strong as iron—for iron breaks and smashes everything—and as iron breaks things to pieces, so it will crush and break all the others. Just as you saw that the feet and toes were partly of baked clay and partly of iron, so this will be a divided kingdom, yet it will have some of the strength of iron in it, even as you saw iron mixed with clay. As the toes were partly iron and partly clay, so this kingdom will be partly strong and partly brittle. And just as you saw the iron mixed with baked clay, so the people will be a mixture and will not remain united, any more than iron mixes with clay. In the days of those kings, the God of heaven will setup a kingdom that will never be destroyed, nor will it be left to another people. It will crush all those kingdoms and bring* *them to an end, but it will itself endure forever. This is the meaning of the vision of the rock cut out of a mountain, but not by human hands—a rock that broke the iron, the bronze, the clay, the silver and the gold to pieces".*

Now before we start going over the different kingdoms, I would like to first point out parts of the statue in their different components. The head is pretty much cut dry and to the point, there was only one ruler and king of this empire. Daniel said that this was the Babylonian empire; which consists of the territories of modern day Turkey, Syria, Lebanon, Iraq, and Iran. Babylon is also the smallest of these four empires.

Also that in Bible prophesy "beast of the field and Birds of the air," always represents demonic (evil) types of spirits. Keep that in mind, because they do influence all these other kingdoms. And lastly, it seems that it is human nature to want to rule the world. These kingdoms at some time have ruled the world, not just part of it. It stands to reason that they were just a strong and mighty power on the earth. There were other kingdoms on the earth but weaker ones. Similar to how the United States, China, Japan, Korea, and Russia are always trying to jockey for the same super power status.

The chest and "arms" of silver, the two arms by several scholars are believed to represent one arm for the Medes and the other arm the Persian's. The Bible does confirm this through two kings; Cyrus and Darius. In this kingdom both the Medes and the Persians became one to form the one world ruling kingdom. This empire consisted of the above territories plus, parts of central Asia, Pakistan, Afghanistan, Saudi Arabia, Jordon, Israel, Egypt and Libya.

The belly and thighs of bronze empire, a solid mid-section was ruled by one king; Alexander the Great. Both the Medo-Persia and Grecian empires ruled the same areas as above.

The legs of iron lasted the longest, even if you combined the total of the first three world powers together, Rome lasted the longest and does take up most of the body of this statue. Iron is the cheapest yet it is also the strongest of all the other metals. Now according to Daniel the Roman Empire will last until the Second coming of

Christ. Since there are two legs this tells me that the Roman Empire has either split or divided under a different title or name; we were not given any further identification. The only known land mass of that time was the Middle Eastern, Asian and African territories. During the Roman empire, they controlled the same areas plus the following: western Europe, England, Britain, Spain, France, Greece, Middle East, North Africa, Italy, Portugal, Belgium, Netherland, Germany, Switzerland, Austria, Hungary, Yugoslavia, Albania, Romania and Bulgaria. Each of the following empires kept growing as the civilized world kept growing as well. Most of these countries did not exist until last century.

None of these empires had to go very far to conquer any of the tribes, nations, or cultures (ethnic groups). Each of these kingdoms lived and had their part in these following empires as they ruled during their time periods. Each empire took over or repossessed the same houses. Of course they would remodel and modify it to their own liking, in most cases to rebuild to their own majestic ideas and gods.

These different kingdoms that will have world dominants, of the known world in their time; head of gold is Babylon (B.C. 605-539) an eighty-seven year reign, the arms and breast of silver is Medo-Persian (B.C. 539-331) a 209 year reign, thighs of brass is Grecian (Greece) (B.C. 331-168) an184 year reign, legs of iron is Roman (B.C. 168-A.D. 476) an 622 year reign [These years of empire rule are close estimates since the years can be debatable].

At the end of the first Roman era, countries and nations started forming and spreading throughout this continent. So it was the end of a great Roman empire but not the end of the people as a culture. They all started out as tribal communities, such as the Germanic tribe as far back as B.C. 500 which later became Germany, which was established during the second Reich (Ottoman Empire) in the 1870's. The same would be true for France, Italy, England, and Britain, each of them had their own area of the world; they were also a part of the iron legs. There has always been a world power, so what happened after A.D. 476? Out of these four empires only two still exist today to carry their original names: Greece and Roman (Rome, Italy). The others became weak or smaller, or came under a different name, or ended up like Babylon and the Medo-Persian that were left in ruins.

The start of the Holy Roman Empire was in A.D. 800 when Pope Leo III crowned Charlemagne and several others after him, as they reigned by different Pope's, this lasted until 1806.

It was Pope Leo III that said on that day, the 25th of December, that the Roman Empire had now become the Holy Roman Empire (in A.D. 800). Charlemagne was not a Roman, he was a German Chancellor or king. This was the first time in the history of the world where politics and religion had been officially mixed and the beginning of the feet of iron and clay from the statue.

Charlemagne (742-814) was also known as Charles the Great, a medieval emperor who ruled much of Western Europe from 768-814. In 771 he became king of the Franks, a Germanic tribe in present day Belgium, France, Luxembourg, Netherlands and Western Germany.

From A.D. 800 to the present, the world has become part of the feet of clay and iron mixture. The ten toes have started to form; which will be the ten kings of the world ruling the ten divided regions. **Daniel 2:41-43** explains it as:

> *"Just as you saw that the feet and toes were partly of baked clay and partly of iron, so this will be a divided kingdom, yet it will have some of the strength of iron in it, even as you saw iron mixed with clay. As the toes were partly iron and partly clay, so this kingdom will be partly strong and partly brittle. And just as you saw the iron mixed with baked clay, so the people will be a mixture and will not remain united, any more than iron mixes with clay."*

The majority of the theologian elites believe that the clay portion represents a religious part, which I believe. Though I cannot find anything in the Bible to confirm this thinking. There has been an obvious assumption that may or may not be true. Due to the vast diversity and cultural indifferences, historically the Roman Empire was destroyed within its borders and not from an invading army.

There is another possibility about the clay being mortar or concrete. We did not start building with this substance until the mid-late first century. It was the Romans that created the use of concrete in construction of their buildings and roads. In modern times it has been common to build with both of these elements.

As of November 2009 the Revived Holy Roman Empire has become officially established. The European Union had failed to pass a Constitution Resolution for this Revived Holy Roman Empire since the early 1990's, through their 27 nation members at this time, which would have been very difficult to accomplish. So they found an easier way to make it pass through a treaty, instead of the individual people from each of these countries having a vote for the Constitution or an Amendment Ratification which makes it impossible for approval. Giving up one's sovereignty is not something any nation is willing to do. A treaty is only signed by and goes through the Heads of State and not the population; hence the Lisbon Treaty.

The final part of Nebuchadnezzar dream; Daniel further explains in verses **Daniel 44-45**.

> *"In the time of those kings, the God of heaven will set up a kingdom that will never be destroyed, nor will it be left to another people. It will crush all those kingdoms and bring them to an end, but it will itself endure forever. This is the meaning of the vision of the rock cut out of a mountain, but not by human hands—a rock that broke the iron, the bronze, the clay, the silver and the gold to pieces."*

Some theologians believe that this rock will be the battle at Armageddon, destroying all the kingdoms of the world once and for all, making way for the everlasting throne of Jesus Christ. This is not just speaking about Jesus Christ millennial (1000 year reign), but His forever and eternal dominion.

In **chapter seven**, Daniel shares his dream of four types of animals and was given an explanation of the four beasts and these horns; (the dream) verses **3-8, 11-14**;

> *"The <u>first</u> was like a **lion**, and it had the **wings of an eagle**. I watched until its **wings were torn off** and it was lifted from the ground so that it **stood on two feet like a man**, and the **heart of a man was given it**. And there before me was a <u>second</u> beast, which looked like a <u>bear</u>. It was raised up on one of its sides, and it had three ribs in its mouth between its teeth. It was told, Get up*

*and eat your fill of flesh! After that, I looked and there before me was another <u>third</u> beast, one that looked like a **leopard**. And on its back it had **four wings like those of a bird**. This beast **had four heads**, and it was given authority to rule. After that, in my vision at night I looked, and there before me was a <u>fourth</u> **beast** <u>terrifying</u> and <u>frightening</u> and <u>very powerful</u>. It had **large iron teeth**; it **crushed** and **devoured** its **victims** and **trampled** underfoot whatever was left. <u>It was different from all the former beasts</u>, and it had **ten horns**… Then I continued to watch because of the <u>boastful</u> <u>words the horns was speaking</u>. I kept looking until the <u>beast was</u> <u>slain</u> and its <u>body destroyed</u> and <u>thrown into the blazing fire</u>. (**The other beasts had been stripped of their authority, but were allowed to live for a period of time**.) In my vision at night I looked, and there before me was **one like a Son of Man, coming with the clouds of heaven**. He approached the Ancient of Days and was led into his presence. **He was given authority, glory** and **sovereign power**, **all peoples**, **nations** and men **of every language worshiped Him**. <u>His dominion</u> is an **everlasting dominion** that <u>will not pass</u> <u>away</u>, and His kingdom is one that <u>will never be destroyed</u>.*"

The interpretation verses **17, 23-25**

*"The four great beasts are **four kingdoms** that will rise from the earth. But the saints of the Most High will receive the kingdom and will possess it forever yes, for ever and ever… He gave me this explanation: The **fourth beast** is a fourth kingdom that will appear on earth. It will be **different from all the other kingdoms** and will devour the whole earth, trampling it down and crushing it. The ten horns are **ten kings** who **will come from this kingdom**. After them another king will arise, different from the earlier ones; he will subdue three kings. He will speak against the Most High and oppress his saints and **try** to change the set times and the law. The saints will be handed over to him for **a time, times and half a time**.*"

Though it is not a complete interpretation, the only understanding is that these beastly animals are kingdoms and the horns are kings; it doesn't give us clarity of who they actually are. This vision is more descriptive about the Endtimes and has shared some important key players. God is a purposeful God, every detail has a reason. But also God's way may have different meanings but not in prophecies. Some scholars say that the Roman Empire has not completely fallen away. There seems to be a raiment that passes from kingdom to kingdom. This is why there are some similarities between them, such as greed, pride, arrogance, and destruction.

Now while other scholars believe that the lion represents Babylon, the bear represents Medes-Persian, the four heads of the leopard represents Grecian generals and the terrifying frightful beast representing the Roman Empire. This reasoning makes absolutely no sense to me. During this vision the Babylonian Empire fell and Daniel was presently under the rule of the Medo-Persian Empire. There is just no bases for a past or present prophesy, this is about future events. The second and seventh chapters are two distinctly different dreams or visions. The second chapter statue was dealing with the soon immediate future kingdoms. While chapter seven was dealing with the End of Age or Endtime nations. There is no just bases for a past or present prophecies, this will be about up and coming future events.

Each of these empires has ruled over the same areas, but has grown each time the scepter has been handed over. Each previous kingdom became or was a part of the kingdom of the previous empire. Why would John's Revelation have all four of the same beasts showing up in his vision still alive and well, if by the time of his writings three out of the four Empires have already fallen or passed away? The first three were stripped of their authority and are allowed to live for a time period, so they still exist just not with any authority.

The fourth one is the only one that is going to be destroyed and thrown into the blazing fire. Unless by now they are now carrying a different name or title. Babylon is now Iraq, the Medo-Persia (the prince of Persia) was changed to Iran, and Grecian has become Greece. I also don't see how the statue in chapter two can *completely* mesh together with this vision any other way.

But what about the eagle's wing that came off the lion and then stood on two feet and a heart or a mind of a man was given to it, and the four wings of a bird (fowl) on the leopard's back and why the four heads of this leopard? John's writing says nothing about these wings or the man. Could it be that these are two different nations that were not born yet in Daniel's prophecy? And has become a separate State or Country in John's prophecy? Some theologians believe that the eagle and the man are one and the same, the United States of America. We cannot just simply discard these things. Those things are just as important and require some justifiable response. It is called attention to details. Their reasoning for this is that the United States has two symbols describing this Nation, the Bald Eagle and Uncle Sam. The bird of a fowl or Rooster symbol represents France. The four heads of the Leopard is *Not* the four generals from Greece, but a number of times the same kingdom rose and fell from power. Some will say these four heads were the four generals that inherited the Grecian empire from Alexander the Great, after his death. In Bible prophecy, heads of a beast would be too big to resemble any one person. They represent a kingdom and the many times that kingdom has risen and fallen. An individual king or leader would be a much smaller part of the body.

Many scholars seem to overlook the two different wings and the man given the heart or mind. The only logical reasoning in order to fit this prophecy is that they represent the countries of France and the United States. I have not found any other evidence to support otherwise.

Daniel was overly concerned about wanting to know more about the Fourth kingdom. This Fourth kingdom will be nothing like any other kingdom from the history of our planet. It will be a time of great turmoil, suffering, and distress the world has never known before.

In **chapter eight**, the vision of the ram and the goat, verses **Daniel 8: 19-26** interpretation; *He (Gabriel) said: "I am going to tell you what will happen <u>later in the Time of Wrath</u>, because the <u>vision concerns the appointed Time of the End</u>. The two-horned ram that you saw represents the kings of Media and Persia (Iran). The shaggy goat is the king of Greece, and the large horn between his eyes is the first king. The four horns that replaced the one that was broken off represent four kingdoms that will emerge from his nation but will not have the same power. In the latter part of their reign, when rebels have become completely wicked, a stern-faced king, a master of intrigue, will arise. He will become very strong, but not by his own power. He will cause astounding devastation and will* *succeed in whatever he does. He will destroy the mighty men and the holy people. He will cause deceit to prosper, and he will consider himself superior. When they feel secure, he will destroy many and take his stand against the prince of princes. Yet he will be destroyed, but not by human power. The vision of the evenings and mornings that has been given you is true, but seal up the vision, for it concerns the distant future.*"

This prophecy is for the far distant future, at the End of the Time and of God's Wrath. The Bible refers to the term Latter Days as the outpouring from Pentecost (in Acts) and forward (to The End). The two horns on the Ram are classified as the Medes and Persia referring to the two horns as a divided kingdom, known as present day Iran. The goat is the kingdom of Greece not a king. This was a miss translation from the Hebrew language to English, it would not make sense for the goat and the horns to both represent the same thing. God is simply not a God of confusion. The first king (the large horn) in modern times could have been Otto Friedrich Ludwig from 1832-1862. Since this prophecy is speaking about a different time line of perilous proportions. The following four kings could have been; George I from 1863-1913, Constantine I from 1913-1917 & 1920-1922, Alexander I from 1917-1920 and George II from 1922-1924, 1935-1941 & 1944-1947. So regardless this prophecy is not referring to Alexander the Great and his four generals, they were in a nearer future to Daniel's period (B.C. era). It also states that four actual kingdoms will stand or rise up out of this nation.

Not that this nation will be split four ways, shared as one and reign at the same time. They will not have the same strength or authoritative power as their predecessor. I have not found anything explaining what "broken off" means in this passage. Other than Greece, struggling and were having had a lot of political and governmental issues. The latter part of this scripture many researchers believe that the wicked, sternface, master of intrigue, very strong not by his own power, devastating and destroying the mighty and the holy people, deceitful with a false sense of security will be antichrist. He will be an evil dictator, but he may not be *the* antichrist. Unless we have forgotten our history, this could as an example have described Hitler to a tee. The actual antichrist will try to rule the world, not just a country, similar to what Germany tried to do. This has nothing to do with Greece. I was just using that as an example. Keep in mind that there will always be a spirit type of antichrist that (tries to) control our thoughts (**I John 4:1-6, II Thessalonians 2:7**). The other thing we need to take into account are the differences in the land masses. The Grecian Empire was much larger than present day Greece, from the India border westward to parts of Europe and Egypt. This madman may come from any part of this region. This could have described Napoleon, as well. At any event, I as well as other theologians believe that Gabriel was speaking about a much later time.

I was told by a respected friend of mine several years ago that there are supposed to be three different antichrists at three different time periods in the flesh. The first was Napoleon, the second was Hitler, the third one is yet to come. Some scholars believe that he is alive and well on planet earth. The last one to come soon will fill the above descriptions completely.

> In **chapter nine,** Gabriel explains to Daniel the Seventy "Sevens", verses **24-27;** *"Seventy sevens are decreed for your people and your holy city to finish transgression, to put an end to sin, to atone for wickedness, to bring in everlasting righteousness, to seal up vision and prophecy and to anoint the Most High. Know and understand this: from the issuing of the decree to restore and rebuild Jerusalem until the Anointed One, the Ruler, comes, there will be seven sevens, and sixty-two sevens. It will be rebuilt with streets and a trench, but in Times of Trouble. After the sixty-two sevens, the Anointed One will be cut off and will have nothing. The people of the Ruler who will come will destroy the city and the sanctuary. The end will come like a flood: War will continue until the end, and desolations have been decreed. He will confirm a covenant with many for one seven. In the middle of the seven he will put an end to sacrifice and offering. And on a wing of the temple he will set up an abomination that causes desolation, until the end that is decreed is poured out on him."*

The Seventy Weeks or 490 years also known as Seventy Sevens, pertain strictly to God's chosen people, the Jewish Nation. It is also important to note that these Weeks have nothing to do with the Gentiles or the Church. It will only cover the time period when the Jews are, by God's permission, dwelling as a people in their own original land. It does not cover any other time frames while they are dispersed throughout the world. These Weeks have been divided into three parts; seven weeks or forty-nine years, sixty-two weeks or 434 years and one week or seven years. In accordance to the Word of God a day has always equaled a year (**Numbers 14:34** and **Ezekiel 4:6**).

The decree to rebuild the temple started the timer of these seventy weeks. This took place during the Medes-Persian Empire in B.C. 445, you can read about it in **Nehemiah chapter two** (14th of March). From that point until the Messiah's grand triumphal entry (**Matthew 21:8-11, Mark 11:8-11, Luke 19:36-44,** and **John 12:16-19**), (2nd of April) will total 483 years (49 + 434 = 483 years). But there is a problem with this figure, B.C. 445 + A.D. 30 = 475 years, a difference of eight years.

There are different types of lengths of years we need to figure into account such as, Lunar years = 354 days, Calendar years = 360 days, Solar years = 365 days, and Julian = 365.25 days. In God's Word He uses 360 days as a Prophetical chronology Calendar year (**Genesis 7:11-13; 8:3-4**).

Now the only way to do this math is to break it down into steps because it can be quite confusing. The 475 years we got from B.C. 445 to A.D. 30 are sixty-four Solar years (365 each). We still have to add the one year missing going from B.C. to A.D. bringing the value to 476 years. We multiply 476 by 365 days in a solar year, equals 173,740 days, now add 119 days for the leap years that brings the total to 173,859. Now we add the 20 days from March 14th (the decree) to April 2nd (Palm Sunday) our total balance becomes 173,879 days. From there we divide 173,879 by 360 (days in Prophetical chronology calendar) = 483 years, which is also sixty-nine weeks of Daniel. There is no break between the first and second set of weeks.

Once the Anointed One has been cut off, the Weeks have stopped and the Israelites have dispersed. Wars and conflicts will continue for the Jewish people to the End. Once the Israelites return back home there will be a signed Decree, which will restart the final last Week. A peace covenant will be confirmed with antichrist for seven years (one Week), which he voids in the middle of the Week (three and a half years), stopping all sacrifices.

The Wing in the temple most scholars believe might be regarded as the Mercy Seat. In the Old Testament the Ark of the Covenant had two Winged creatures on the Ark, this was also called the Mercy Seat of God. Antichrist will cause abomination and desolation one last time, since this has happened at least three other times—Antiochus B.C. 168, Caligula A.D. 40…some suggested again with Nero in A.D. 70 prior to the destruction. The abomination and desolations in the past were given in the form of a statue only, never as an actual person in the flesh. They were also not the actual Antichrist, only an influential agent in his spirit. The Antichrist to come will be manifested in the flesh. At God's timing His decree will still stand and He will pour out on him, what is coming to him.

In **chapter eleven**, verses **36-45**; *"The king will do as he pleases. He will exalt and magnify himself above every god and will say unheard of things against the God of gods. He will be successful until the Time of Wrath is completed, for what has been determined must take place. He will show no regards for the gods of his fathers or for the one desired by women, nor will he regard any gods, but will exalt himself above them all. Instead of them, he will honor a god of fortresses; a god unknown to his fathers he will honor with gold and silver, with precious stones and costly gifts. He will attack the mightiest fortresses with the help of a foreign god and will greatly honor those who acknowledge him. He will make them rulers over many people and will distribute the land at a price. At the Time of the End the king of the South will engage him in battle, and the king of the North will storm out against him with chariots and cavalry and a great fleet of ships. He will invade many countries and sweep through them like a flood. He will also invade the beautiful Land. Many countries will fall, but Edom, Moab and the leaders of Ammon will be delivered from his hand. He will extend his power over many countries, Egypt will not escape. He will gain control* *of the treasures of gold and silver and all the riches of Egypt, with the Libyans and Nubians (northern Sudan and southern Egypt) in submission. But reports from the east and the north will alarm him, and he will set out in a great rage to destroy and annihilate many. He will pitch his royal tents between the seas at the beautiful holy mountain. Yet he will come to his end, and no one will help him."*

There are a lot of conflicts as to whether or not this chapter should be included as part of the End of Age prophecies. Some believe this prophecy was fulfilled by the time of the transition into the New Testament, and including up to the first two decades. The first half of this chapter (vs. **1-28**), according to most theologians, they believe this prophecy was dealing with the near future of Daniel's time. It was foretelling of the rise of the next Empire, Alexander the Great. The second half of this chapter (vs. **29-45**) was describing the Roman Empire. Not every ruthless king, will be "the" actual antichrist, this king can describe the life and times of Herod. I believe this is something that is yet to come.

The phrase "the desire of women" has been misunderstood, taken out of content indicating that he will have no desire for women. Leaving people to think he will be celibate or a homosexual. That is not what is being said. The proper word text should be; the hope of every religious Jewish woman that she might be the mother of the promised Messiah (or to be able to carry the offspring of the false messiah or antichrist). For the sake of this book, I won't be covering these details. Regardless the nation of Israel has had its full share of troubles and hardships in their long history.

This description can also fit well with all of the other Caesars of the Roman Empire. These emperors have always claimed divinity and demanded worship as their god. I believe there are several key phrases in this scripture that would raise a red flag. The "Time of Wrath" would indicate a possible <u>Endtime prophesy</u> yet to be fulfilled. There is also the kings from the South and the North that will war against him at the "Time of the End". The mentioning of the "Beautiful Land" refers to Israel which did not become a nation until May 1948. I believe this evil dictator is yet to come.

Many do believe that this deals with an Endtime conflict. Some have assumed that this conflict will come from every direction including from the West. **Ezekiel chapters 38 and 39** gives more details of these armies and where they came from. There is no mentioning throughout the Bible of any force coming from the West, only from the North, South, and East. It is all about the location of Israel, from the West   is the Mediterranean Sea (Pacific Ocean). There is no indication in the Bible that the United States would be involved in making any war with Israel. Several theologians and I do believe it would possibly be a war between the half-brothers, the descendants of Ishmael (Islam) and Isaac (Hebrews), since the countries coming to do battle are 99 percent Muslims.

> In **chapter twelve**, verses **1-12**; *"There will be a time of distress such as has not happened from the beginning of nations until then. But at that time your people—every one whose name is found written in the book—will be delivered. Multitudes who will sleep in the dust of the earth will awake: some to <u>everlasting life</u>, others to shame and <u>everlasting contempt</u>. Those who are wise will shine like the brightness of the heavens, and those who lead many to righteousness, like the stars forever and ever. But you, Daniel, close up and seal the words of the scroll until the Time of the End. Many will go here and there to <u>increase knowledge</u>. Then I, Daniel, looked, and there before me stood two others, one on this bank of the river and one on the opposite bank. One of them said to the man clothed in linen, who was above the waters of the river. "How long will it be before these astonishing things are fulfilled?" The man clothed in linen, who was above the waters of the river, lifted his right hand and his left hand towards heaven, and I heard him swear by Him who lives forever, saying, "<u>It will be for a time, times and half a time</u>. When the power of the holy people has been finally broken, all these things will be completed." I heard, but I did not understand. So I asked, "My lord what will the outcome of all this be?" He replied, "Go your way, Daniel, because the words are closed up and Sealed until the <u>Time of the End</u>. Many will be purified, made spotless and refined, but the wicked will continue to be wicked. None of the wicked will understand, but those who are wise will understand. "From the*

time that the daily sacrifice is abolished and the abomination that causes desolation is set up, there will be 1,290 days. Blessed is the one who waits for and reaches the End of the 1,335 days."

I have met a lot of distressed people. We have not yet seen what it means to go through a time of distress. The world will get a whole lot uglier and freakier in the coming days. On our worst of days, it will still be our best of days by comparison. There are two groups; one sleeping and one waken; one to everlasting life while the other group was given to everlasting contempt. This looks to be the resurrection of the wheat and the tares from Jesus' parable (**Matthew 13:24-30**). After this Daniel is told to seal up the words until knowledge is increased. The sealing up just means that no more further explanation needs to be added, and that it is for an appointed time. In time these things will be revealed.

The knowledge started to slowly increase by the early 17th and 18th century and picked up a lot of speed during the 19th and 20th century. Most scholars believe that the man that raised his hands to heaven was Jesus. The time, times and half a time (three and a half years) is the timeline for the Great Tribulation, or the days of (Jacob's) sorrow. The power that will finally be broken from God's holy people (Israelites) is their spiritual blindness. They have denied Jesus Christ as the Messiah and God's sacrificial Lamb, they will finally see Him as He is. For the second time Daniel is told to seal these words, it was not meant for Daniel to understand these things.

God is going to bring us all through a purification and refining process. Some theologians and I feel that the Rapture would not happen until this is completed. This is also where many will be separated or fallen away from their faith (**Hebrews 3:12; I Timothy 4:1**). In **Ester 2:12** she went through something similar for one full year—six months purification and six months cleansing—before she was allowed to marry the king. Most scholars believe this as an actual life allegory. We are called the bride of the King and are to be spotless, wearing white garments.

Meanwhile the wicked will continue as they are and still be ignorant and careless of the things going on all around them. The daily sacrifices will stop, whether forcefully or willingly we do not know this for sure. It will also be at this point that the abomination of desolation will happen at the mid-point of 1290 days or three and a half years of the Great Tribulation.

I have found nothing in the bible to shed any clarity to the 1335 days. There is a forty-five day difference between these two figures. Since Daniel said, "Blessed is the one who waits and reaches this End." My theory, since the bible does say that Jesus Christ is our "Blessed Hope," is possibly the second coming of our Lord and King (depending on the translation, **Titus 2:13** uses wait, waiting, awaiting, while, expect, expectation or looking for the blessed hope). Armageddon will come about at The End of the three and a half years. It might not start and end in a single day. It may take at least a week just to get all these nations there. Armageddon might not be an easy conflict, it will be an all-out battle, a bloody mess.

The following are parallels that compliments each other between the book of Daniel and the book of Revelation:

They both saw the world's final kingdom	Dan. 7:9-26	Rev. 17:11-14
They both saw a time frame of seven years	Dan. 9:27	Rev. 1:2;13:5
They both saw the final rule for forty-two months	Dan. 12:7	Rev. 12:14
They both saw the rise of a final dictator	Dan. 8:23-25	Rev. 13:1-2
They both saw a final kingdom described as a beast	Dan. 7:7	Rev. 13:1-2
They both saw ten kings accompanying the beast	Dan. 7:27	Rev. 17:12

They both saw a time of great tribulation on the earth	Dan. 12:1	Rev. 7:14
They both saw great trouble for Israel and Jews	Dan. 12:1	Rev. 12:17
They both saw Michael the Archangel intervene	Dan. 12:1	Rev. 12:7
They both saw into the throne room of God	Dan. 7:9	Rev. 4:2
They both saw thousands around the throne of God	Dan. 7:10	Rev. 5:11
They both saw books opened in heavenly judgment	Dan. 7:10	Rev. 20:12
They both saw the return of the Messiah	Dan. 7:13	Rev. 19:11
They both saw the Messiah coming in the cloud	Dan. 7:13	Rev. 1:7
They both saw the beast burning in flames	Dan. 7:11	Rev. 19:20
They both saw the saints reigning in Christ's Kingdom	Dan. 7:22	Rev. 20:4
They both saw an everlasting Kingdom without end	Dan. 7:27	Rev. 21:1-4

There are other EndTime scriptures and books that I will not cover in this book that deals with the ancient Old Testament tribes. I also don't want to make this book any larger than it has already gotten. My desire is for this book to be an easy and manageable read. Also to allow you to continue your own study and quest for the truth. For continued reading on the subject, in part or as a whole, they are as the following books in the Old Testament:

Esther (a real life allegory)

Ezra

Nehemiah

Isaiah 2, 11, 13-14, 24-27, 65

Jeremiah 49

Ezekiel 36-43

Psalms 83

Joel

Zephaniah

Zechariah

CHAPTER EIGHT

BABYLON IS NO MORE

Revelation 18:1-3 *"I saw another angel coming down from heaven. He had great authority, and the earth was illuminated by his splendor. With a mighty voice he shouted: "Fallen! Fallen is Babylon the great! She has become a home of demons and a haunt for every unclean and detestable bird. For every nations have drunk the maddening wine of her adulteries. The kings of the earth committed adultery with her, and the merchants of the earth grew rich from her excessive luxuries."*

THIS MIGHTY ANGEL is declaring the Final End of this mystery (new) Babylon, which is the sinful capital city of the whole earth. This huge city will be the dwelling place for every kind of evil desire. This city will be so full of selfish greed to fulfill each and every wimble of an individual's itchy thought in their hearts and minds. Judgment has come down to this city and has been found guilty of all their abominations. There were cultic activities of every pagan god known, to satisfy everyone's evil desires. These people will be influenced by demonic spirits. There will be excessive buying and selling of every kind of stuff imaginable, drugs, alcohol, foods, and people. Wealth and luxury will be plentiful, with a false sense of confidence in the world.

In the Bible there are a lot of type of, shadows and symbols throughout. These detestable birds are just one of them. They are considered an evil demonic spiritual influence, same as the beasts of the field. Mystery Babylon or New Babylon will not be at the original site of the Old Babylon. The Bible clearly states that it will remain uninhabitable and desolate since it fell during the BCE period **(Isaiah 13:20).**

During, in the 1980's Saddam Hussein attempted to rebuilt Babylon at the original site, which he barely got started. It was started but was never even close to being finished. Then the Gulf War broke out and he became a fugitive, and eventually executed for his crimes.

There are several possible hints and beliefs about the actual location. There might actually be a reason why it is called Mystery Babylon, we might not ever know the location. Most theologians believe it will be a large coastal city for importing and exporting goods through merchant shipping. I have heard of four cities in the United States that could fit this bill, San Diego, San Francisco, Miami, and New York. I believe this to be totally false because there is no evidence to support such a thing. It has to be located around Europe or Middle Eastern areas.

In **Revelation chapter 17,** It refers to the seven heads as seven hills on which the harlot sits. Many believe that this would be the location for Mystery Babylon. Most theologians say that Mystery Babylon will be within the original Roman Empire territory as stated earlier in this book. Since the animal symbolism was part of the Roman Empire; the Lion, the Bear, and the Leopard, common sense reasoning would likely conclude that the New Babylon would also be geographically in the same area.

> **Revelation 18:4-8** *"I heard another voice from heaven saying: 'Come out of her, My people, so that you will not share in her sins, so that you will not receive any of her plagues; for her sins are piled up to heaven, and God has remembered her crimes.' Give back to her as she has given; pay her back double for what she has done. Mix her double portion from her own cup. Give her as much torture and grief as the glory and luxury she gave herself. In her heart she boasts, 'I sit as queen; I am not a widow.' Therefore in one day her*

*plagues will overtake her: death, mourning and famine. She will
be consumed by fire, for mighty is the Lord God who judges her."*

This other authoritative voice calls out to God's people (the
Tribulation Saints) to separate from the behaviors of this society. Like
the days of Lot they will have to just leave, without looking back. We
are to always communicate the Gospel of Jesus Christ in our everyday
life. But at this point there will be no reasoning with them. We are
only the messengers! The fallen world or people will still have to make
their own choices. There will be a time where they will need to just
walk away as they can only do so much. That is exactly what Jesus
did in His earthly Ministry. Christianity was never to be forced upon
anyone. Nor are we to argue over the truth, like a lot of Christians
tend to do. This would be an example of the blind leading the blind.
We can debate people if necessary, as long as there is a chance to be
open minded and a hope for reasoning. But it must be done in love
and compassion.

This will be a warning sign to stop, turn and come to follow
God's holy and righteous ways. If they continue through Babylon's
path they will suffer the same fate. Like the cup of God's Wrath that
eventual becomes full, likewise her sins have piled to the high heavens.
There is no turning back from these wicked ways. There will always
be a judgment for our choices and actions. One thing is for sure—
God never forgets as her unrepentant crimes are remembered. Like
in **Zechariah chapter nine** God will pay double portions for our
troubles, but will also pay the opposite, instead of blessings it will
be a judgment. This mixed drink will be perfectly portioned, no
more and no less than what she deserves. She regards herself highly
as in a position of arrogant royalty. Some commentators say that these
might be the same plagues from the seven bowls poured out in **chapter 16**, or they can be something totally different all together. Her
doom will come as quickly as in one day. In the end the inhabitants
will be shocked as she is over taken by fire and destroyed. In the same
way that we the church (true followers) of Christ are known as the
Bride of Christ, so are the unbelievers and followers are known as

the bride of Satan. Regardless, you are someone's bride, it is a choice. Choose wisely.

> **Revelation 18:9-13** *"When the kings of the earth who committed adultery with her and shared her luxury see the smoke of her burning, they will weep and mourn over her. Terrified of her torment, they will stand far off and cry: Woe! Woe, O great city, O Babylon, city of power! In one hour your doom has come!" The merchants of the earth will weep and mourn over her because no one buys their cargoes any more—cargoes of gold, silver, precious stones and pearls; fine linen, purple, silk and scarlet cloth; every sort of citron wood, bronze, iron and marble; cargoes of cinnamon and spice, of incense, myrrh and frankincense, of wine and olive oil fine flour and wheat; cattle and sheep; horses and carriages; and bodies and souls of men."*

All of the leaders of the earth that took part in the abominable things of God will see the destruction of Babylon, they will cry out in amazement. This city will be known as the central part of the world for importing and exporting goods. It will be like the great depression all over again, only a whole lot worst. They will be seeing their wealth and livelihood going up in smoke. It will be a horrible sight to those who have put their trust in things, instead of God. Everything imaginable could have been purchased at this powerful city, including sex and servant slaves, but now it has come to an end. All of these material things will either be burned during the fire or stored somewhere, with the exception of the livestock and slaves. They could have also suffered death as part of these plagues. I believe as do other commentators that the bodies and souls of men were slaves, possibly captured Christians or someone unable to pay off a debt. The word for "men" can also refer to mankind or humankind, such includes women. This might also sound like human trafficking.

> **Revelation 18:14-20** *"They will say, 'The fruit you longed for is gone from you. All your riches and splendor have vanished, never to be recovered.' The merchants who sold these things and gained their wealth from her will stand far off, terrified at her torment. They will weep and mourn and cry out: Woe! Woe O great city,*

dressed in fine linen, purple and scarlet, and glittering with gold, precious stones and pearls! In one hour such great wealth has been brought to ruin!' Every sea captain, and all who travel by ship, the sailors, and all who earn their living from the sea, will stand far off. When they see the smoke of her burning, they will exclaim, 'Was there ever a city like this great city?' They will throw dust on their heads, and with weeping and mourning cry out: "Woe! Woe, O great city, where all who had ships on the sea became rich through her wealth! In one hour she has been brought to ruin! Rejoice over her, O heaven! Rejoice, saints and apostles and prophets! God has judged her for the way she treated you."'

The inhabitants are the ones talking about the fruitful greed that has been removed and disappeared never to return. It will be these corporations that will suffer the greatest lost. Their so called good life has now taken a turn towards judgment, fear and dread has overcome them. In unbelief they started to reminisce of the city's beauty. Then, how in a matter of just one day (an hour) it has become a pile of rubble. [In Bible prophecy one day equals one year and an hour equals one day.] This verse talks about sea captains and sailors making a living, indicating that this mighty city is in fact close to a large body of water. So could this be any city around coastal waters? Some look to New York City to fit this description, but they are wrong. The answer was in **chapter 17**, a city with seven hills. Both the Old Babylon and the New Babylon will not be at the same location. But they will be at the same geographical area. We would have to go back and understand the original structure of these empire's land masses. The Roman Empire has over lapped the Babylonian Empire, which almost tripled in size, each empire got bigger as they dominated. Italy was occupied as part of the Roman Empire. The city of Rome is surrounded by seven hills and is also close to a large body of water. We as believers in Christ can rejoice over her demise because of the ill treatment we were given because of her abominable ways.

Revelation 18:21-24 *"Then a mighty angel picked up a boulder the size of a large millstone and threw it into the sea, and said:*

'With such violence the great city of Babylon will be thrown down, never to be found again. The music of harpists and musicians, flute players and trumpeters, will never be heard in you again. No workman of any trade will ever be found in you again. The sound of a millstone will never be heard in you again. The light of a lamp will never shine in you again. The voice of bridegroom and bride will never be heard in you again. Your merchants were the world's great men. By your magic spell all the nations were led astray. In her was found the blood of prophets and of the saints, and of all who have been killed on the earth.'"

A millstone is what was used to grind grain in the Old Testament; they were enormous and weighing several tons. Basically this mighty angel was saying, Babylon or anything like her will never be built or seen again. This could also be the same large stone in **Daniel chapter two** that was thrown down and crushed the metal statue.

The life style described here sounded like a partying place. There was all kinds of music for all types of people. I believe that the people were drawn to her hypnotic brainwashing, never wanting to leave. Usually where there was music you would be able to find any and all kinds of drugs, alcohol, and prostitution or orgies (influences). Las Vegas is known as sin city yet would not be able to compare to this amusement park of gratification. The temptation in this city will be undiluted and overwhelming. There will be no more job opportunities nor will her beacon of light shine ever again. Wedding ceremonies will no longer be performed by these fake pagan religious priests.

Demonic spells will draw the inhabitants to this location from around the world. A false happiness will cause many to be deceived. Since the foundation of the world Satan has always been behind the causes of the shedding of the innocent blood of children and of God's people. Remember the hearts of many will grow cold, so all this is selfish emotions and feelings.

Revelation 19:1-5 *"I heard what sounded like the roar of a great multitude in heaven shouting: 'Hallelujah! Salvation and glory and power belong to our God, for true and just are His judgments. He has condemned the great prostitute who corrupted the earth by her* *adulteries. He has avenged on her the blood of His servants.' And again they shouted: 'Hallelujah! The smoke from her goes up forever and ever.' The twenty-four elders and the four living creatures fell down and worshiped God, who was seated on the throne. And they cried: 'Amen, Hallelujah!' Then a voice came from the throne saying: 'Praise our God, all you His servants, you who fear Him, both small and great!'"*

This may be the avenging that God told them to wait for a little longer in **chapter six**. Finally God's salvation, glory and true judgment have come. He is now ridding the earth of the corruption and correcting the wrong done to His people. All of heaven is celebrating God's greatness. The smoke from Babylon will continue to go up as a memorial forever. This victory has always been God's and God's alone. He is worthy to be praised.

The word "Amen", according to Thayer's dictionary means; to believe, is faithful, sure, truthful or truly, to speak honestly or as a vow, true as unbelievable or unimaginable. Not to doubt and, as a matter of fact. Most of us know the term "so be it"or so it is, from Strong's exhaustive and Young's analytical concordance; we use that a lot in place of Amen. Jesus used "Verily" in the KJV which can be translated as an unbelievable truth or too good to be true.

Revelation 19:6-10 *"I heard what sounded like a great multitude, like the roar of rushing waters and like loud pearls of thunder, shouting: 'Hallelujah! For our Lord God Almighty reigns. Let us rejoice and be glad and give Him glory! For the wedding of the Lamb has come, and His bride has made herself ready. Fine linen, bright and clean, was given her to wear.' (Fine linen stands for the righteous acts of the saints.) Then the angel said to me, 'Write: Blessed are those who are invited to the wedding supper of the Lamb!' And he added, 'These are the true words of God.' At this I fell at his feet to worship him. But he said to me, do not do it! I am a fellow servant with you and with your brothers who hold to the testimony of Jesus. Worship God! For the testimony of Jesus is the Spirit of Prophecy.'"*

There is a multitude of people honoring and glorifying the Lord our God that reigns forever. This is a worthy marriage celebration between the Lamb (Christ the King) and His bride (the true and pure Church). No one knows for sure how long the wedding will last or if the length is important. But think about this, I do not feel this celebration will by no means be short or a quick event. We will have all eternity, so what would be the rush. All of the believers throughout time waited and looked forward to this gathering. This will go far beyond anything we have ever partaken while on earth. We will meet saints we have heard or read about, or those that were taken from our youth. The bride was finally made ready through the purification and cleansing process.

Some believe this could have been through the persecution and tribulation processes. I believe it to be partially correct. In addition, it would deal personally with each individual's impurity, the sinful nature that some Christian's still entertain. God has always wanted all of you not just part of you. He plans on cleaning up the house and you are that house. I see Him removing a lot of the junk and all of our distractions in our lives. Regardless we cannot be made clean and ready unless there is a process. The true words of God are our testimony as well as our everyday actions. Faith without action is dead (**James 2:14-16**). The angel quickly rebukes John for trying to worship him. We are to never worship anyone or anything above, beyond, or before the Most High Living God; Creator of the heavens and earth.

> **Revelation 19:11-16** *"I saw heaven standing open and there before me was a white horse, whose rider is called Faithful and True. With justice He judges and makes war. His eyes are like blazing fire, and on His head are many crowns. He has a name written on Him that no one knows but He Himself. He is dressed in a robe dipped in blood, and His name is the word of God. The armies of heaven were following Him, riding on white horses and dressed in fine linen, white and clean. Out of His mouth comes a sharp sword with which to strike down the nations. He will rule them with an iron scepter. He treads the winepress of the fury of the **WRATH** of God Almighty. On His robe and on His thigh He has this name written: KING OF KINGS AND LORD OF LORDS."*

After the wedding we prepare to do battle. The rider on the White Horse is our Lord and King, Jesus Christ Himself, aka Faithful. He is the true Judge that will fight, and cause war to those that opposes Him. The many crowns on His head are the many victories He has won, never losing any. A few commenters say that the blood that the robe is dipped in would possibly be the blood of the (innocent's) saints that were martyred for their testimonies. It would be senseless to think it would be His own blood, since He did not have to save Himself. It is believed to be the avenging blood from all the saints. As Christ was our atoning sacrifice, so also the martyred Christians became the living sacrifice of their testimony. His name is the Word of God that became flesh. All of the other riders in heaven are mounted and ready for battle.

Most theologians believe and so do I, that it will all be Jesus in this battle, He won't need our help. While others say we would partake in it. The only weapon mentioned here is the sharp two edged sword from His mouth, which is power and all authority. There are no other details about the heavenly army, other than wearing fine clean white linen; no helmets, no shields, no other swords. But sometimes we need to just show up, like in the days of Gideon (**Judges chapter 7**) or Jehoshaphat (**II Chronicles chapter 20**), and make some (joyful) noise. Christ will be the Ruler of rulers, as well as the only true King and Lord.

He will strike down every nation that is against Him, nor will they rise again. He will carry the iron scepter showing His righteous position and authority. The metaphor of treading the winepress is a common biblical term to picture God's Wrath in action. After the wedding feast in verses 6-10, the final battle is fought. Some scholars believe that the wedding takes place during the last half of the great tribulation period. It fits. The Holy Spirit has already been removed from the earth, which restrained and prevented Satan full access (**II Thessalonians 2:6-7**).

Also the Rapture already happened and was completed. So this great wedding feast may possibly have lasted three and a half years.

Revelation 19:17-21 *"I saw an angel standing in the sun, who cried in a loud voice to all the birds flying in midair, 'Come, gather together for the great supper of God, so that you may eat the flesh of kings, generals, and mighty men, of horses and their riders, and the flesh of all people, free and slave, small and great.' Then I saw the beast and the kings of the earth and their armies gathered together to make war against the rider on the horse and his army. But the beast was captured, and with him the false prophet who had performed the miraculous signs on his behalf. With these signs he had deluded those who had received the mark of the beast and worshiped his image. The two of them were thrown alive into the fiery lake of burning sulfur. The rest of them were killed with the sword that came out of the mouth of the Rider on the horse, and all the birds gorged themselves on their flesh."*

This angel invites all of the birds in the sky to a great feast. They will be able to eat all of the human dead from this victorious battle. There will be no survivors nor will there be any wounded.

The beast was able to manipulate the leaders and their armies to make war and come up against Jesus Christ, thinking they had a chance to win. It was never that the beast actually believed he had a chance of winning. He just hated God's creation so much that it gave him great pleasure (to see) for the people, God's own creation, fight against (Him) God. The beast and false prophet that performed great magic are captured and thrown alive into the lake of fire. The false prophet was so good that he was able to delude many to take the mark and worship the image. Here it clearly states that the rest of the army was killed solely by the sword that came from the mouth of the Rider, Jesus. In the end, the birds got to enjoy the spoils of this slaughter. The war is finally over, Satan and his cohorts will now face eternal damnation and judgment. The manipulations and lies that they told the inhabitants and was believed. Know the truth only then will you be set free (**John 8:32**).

CHAPTER NINE

ALL THINGS NEW

Revelation 20:1-6 *"I saw an angel coming down from heaven, having the key to the Abyss and holding in his hand a great chain. He seized the dragon, That ancient serpent, who is the Devil and Satan, and bound him for a thousand years. He threw him into the Abyss, and locked and sealed it over him, to keep him from deceiving the nations anymore until the thousand years were ended. After that, he must be set free for a short time. I saw thrones on which were seated those who had been given authority to judge. I saw the souls of those who had been beheaded because of their testimony for Jesus and because of the word of God. They had not worshiped the beast or his image and had not received his mark on their foreheads or their hands. They came to life and reigned with Christ a thousand years. (The rest of the dead did not come to life until the thousand years were ended.) This is the first resurrection. Blessed and holy are those who have part in the first resurrection. The second death has no power over them, but they will be priests of God and of Christ and will reign with him for a thousand years."*

THIS MIGHTY ANGEL with the key to the Abyss and chain finally indicates the impending doom due for the devil. Lucifer will not escape his judgments due to him. The time that all true Christians have been waiting and looking for, the day Satan is finally seized and bound, even though it will only be temporarily before it becomes final. He will not be able to get out from this lock and seal to cause anymore chaotic attacks against the nations of the earth. According to God a thousand years is still a very short time (**Psalm 90:4; II Peter 3:8**). For the purposes of God's righteousness he will be set free for a short time, perhaps a thousand years. There is no exact amount of this freedom he will have during this time, the next portion will shed some light on this.

John saw thrones (plural), he did not say (one), twelve, or twenty-four in numbers, like he did in the previous chapters. Many believe these are several countless thrones, the hint being "given authority to judge" (see **I Corinthians 6:2-3**). This can be the countless thrones promised to all believers mentioned in the Bible (**Daniel 7:27; Matthew 25:20-21**)

This is also where most Christians believe that these beheadings will come from a "Guillotine." There is no indication of this method anywhere in the Bible, only common sense tells us that it will be a sharp blade or sword.

There are three interesting theories behind this, one is that this will strike the most fear or terror into people and many will abandon their faith. They would rather breakdown to Satan than to face a gruesome death. The second is it will provide the most thrill and fear for the crowds watching. It is also believed to become a sporting activity as the world watches the execution, similar to the first century persecution by use of an amphitheater, coliseum or large crowds; now we have the internet via youtube. Lastly antichrist might teach that only the heads are evil, because it is their diseased thoughts and minds that continue stubbornly to believe in Jesus.

In this day and age, nothing surprises me. There is a lot of crazy thinking that people want you to believe in and it will continue to get worst. One such crazy way of thinking, I watched on the news. where during a Congressional hearing, one of the Congressmen asked a young lady a simple question, "Can men get pregnant and have abortions?" Her response was, "Yes." Now that is a special kind of stupid. There was another Congressional hearing with a Supreme Court Justice nominee, where she was asked, what are the difference between a man and a woman. Her response (words to the effect of) she couldn't, that it would be too difficult.

According to the historical records of France and their references to the guillotine, no two beheading are exactly alike. Sometimes the severed head would remain alive for up to 30 seconds. In light of the current condition of our world, I believe it will be from a blade of a sword. Whatever the case may be, I just see him wanting to get rid of all the troublemakers. So this does not tell us how they were beheaded. I do disagree with the use of a guillotine theory since the Bible does not mention any type of blade machine. It only clearly states a sword. Remember the Fourth Horseman in **Revelation 6:7** only killed with a sword, a quarter of the earth. This is also very similar to what radical Islam has been doing for centuries. It is cheap, easy, and effective.

At the time of this writing there is only one possible radical culture that fit this description; radical Islamic, the Taliban or ISIS. They have been brutally beating their captives prior to their deaths; most of them were beheaded while some were shot in the head. I believe when the time comes that these beheadings will increase and will be their method of execution. Using the sword is also the cheapest and fastest method of murder. Of all the technical ways to kill, they will resort back to a more primitive method. With only one goal in mind, remove the troublemakers, the Christians.

I do not believe that Satan will be able to "force" you to take his Mark, it has to be a freedom of choice, your will, using fear of death verses life to motivate the person. The bottom line is Satan could not care any less about any of us. His greatest pleasure is getting you and I to deny Christ, which would be one less person in the Kingdom of Heaven. The souls of the beheaded saints, some theologians say this can fit the time in which we are living. There have been more beheadings of Christians in the past few decades to the present than at any other time in recorded history. Of all the ways to kill a person, none are good; this is simply the barbaric nature of ISIS.

These Tribulation saints stood firm and strong in their Faith, and did not give into this beast. Those that have been Raptured or Resurrected will freely reign with Christ forever. This will only be all of the bodies of believers throughout history. Those that remain dead are the ones who will be condemned in the Second Resurrection, which is death. We will be Blessed to be a part of the First Resurrection, which is Life. Finally we will be given the honor to serve and minister as holy priests to God and to Christ (our Creator Father and our Lord Jesus King and Savior) for 1000 years and forever.

> **Revelation 20:7-14** *"When the thousand years are over Satan will be released from his prison and will go out to deceive the nations in the four corners of the earth—Gog and Magog—to gather them for battle. In number they are like the sand on the seashore. They marched across the breadth of the earth and surrounded the camp of God's people, the city He loves. But fire came down from heaven and devoured them. And the devil, who deceived them, was thrown into the lake of burning sulfur, where the beast and the false prophet had been thrown. They will be tormented day and night forever and ever. I saw a great white throne and him who was seated on it. Earth and sky fled from His presence, and there was no place for them. And I saw the dead, great and small, standing before the throne, and books were opened. Another book was opened, which is the book of life. The dead were judged according to what they had done as recorded in the books. The sea gave up the dead that were in it, and death and hades gave up the dead that were in them, and each person was judged according to what he had done. Then death and hades were thrown into the lake of fire. The lake of fire is the second death. If anyone's name was not found written in the Book of Life, he was thrown into the lake of fire".*

Satan and his cohorts will be released from their a short period of time. He will still be able to lie and manipulate the nations of the world. What really saddened and amazes me, is that Lucifer is a great manipulator and deceiver. He did it in a perfect heavenly paradise, where there are no slums, ghettos, or lack of any kind. God did nothing wrong yet Lucifer was able to caused one-third of the angels to follow him in rebellion. When God created a perfect paradise on earth. Again Lucifer was able to cause the first humans to sin against God for no apparent reason. And Jesus did nothing wrong and Lucifer still was able to cause mankind to murder Him. These are considered the inexcusable rebellion. This only shows how powerful his deceptions are and how far gone humanity has gotten.

The northern territory known as Gog and Magog are in reference to the location of Israel. Any direction used in the Bible is central to the nation of Israel. These nations north can be any of the following countries: Lebanon, Syria, Turkey, Russia, Georgia, and Armenia. Northeast we can include as Iraq and Iran. This will be a huge army, too many to count by our standards. They will surround and come up against the Israelites (Israel). Like the battles God fought in the Old Testament, it will be God that will consume this army with fire that has opposed His people. Lucifer is finally thrown into the lake of fire, where he belongs, joining the beast (antichrist) and false prophet. Where they will never be able to leave or be paroled, nor will have any visitors. They will suffer for what they did—forever. God is an all-consuming presence when He shows all things must depart. Actually there are no places to run or hide. This is the second (death) resurrection, the dead are judged for their evil deeds.

There are two types of Judgments, depending on your position; lost and saved or believer and unbeliever. All saved and believers are judged at the Judgment Seat of Christ (**II Corinthians 5:10**). Only the lost and unbelievers are judged at this Great White Throne Judgment. Everyones works are being judged. This trial is only for the damned. There are different levels of rewards in hell as there are in heaven. There are two sets of books opened, one with the details of their life history and the other book, the Book of Life just indicates all the names of the saved believers. There will be no escaping this Court of Justice as everyone will be summoned to appear. God is not the one that is condemning them, they did it to themselves. They can only blame themselves for their actions. Once the trial is over and the sentencing is complete, death and hades are thrown in the lake of fire, to be no more. This finishes the second death, woe to those whose names are not found in the Book of Life. There will be no gray area!

Revelation 21:1-8 *"I saw a new heaven and a new earth, for the first heaven and the first earth had passed away, and there was no longer any sea. I saw the Holy city, the New Jerusalem, coming* *down out of heaven from God, prepared as a bride beautifully dressed for her Husband. And I heard a loud voice from the throne saying, 'Now the dwelling of God is with men, and He will live with them. They will be His people, and God Himself will be with them and be their God. He will wipe every tear from their eyes. There will be no more death or mourning or crying or pain, for the old order of things has passed away.' He who was seated on the throne said, 'I am making everything new!' Then He said, 'Write this down, for these words are trustworthy and true.' He said to me: 'It is done. I Am the Alpha and the Omega, the Beginning and the End. To him who is thirsty I will give to drink without cost from the spring of the water of life. He who overcomes will inherit all this, and I will be his God and he will be My son. But the cowardly, the unbelieving, the vile, the murderers, the sexually immoral, those who practice magic arts, the idolaters and all liars—their place will be in the fiery lake of burning sulfur. This is the second death.'"*

John was the first and only one to witness the birth of the New Heaven and New Earth. The first heaven and earth was destroyed (cleansed of all unrighteousness) by fire. John does not share any details regarding the New Earth. His focus is on New Jerusalem (**Isaiah 65:17-19; 66:22**). So we do not know much about the characteristic of this New Earth. I believe there will be some similarities as well as some (major) differences. The term John uses is singular, meaning one heaven, not all three of the heavens. Planet earth is part of the 1st heaven; they are one and the same. In this new model there will be no use for any large bodies of water. The New Jerusalem in all her splendor comes down from heaven, taking her rightful place on earth, like a bride on her wedding day. Now God will come and dwell with His people, which are what He has always desired from the foundation of the world. It has always been about a relationship between the Creator and His creation, but our choices and sinfulness prevented it from happening. There will be no more suffering or sickness (emotional, physical or mental traumas)! We will never die, death is now power-less, it was thrown in the lake of fire. These are the old order of things and will be no more. There is now a new order of business, making everything better. With this new order comes unspeakable unknowing pure love, joy, peace and happiness. The trustworthy and true words, *"It Is Finished, completed, done. He is the author (starter) and finisher of our faith. He is all in all one. He is the Great I AM.* (**Exodus 3:14**)" The Christ is still calling those who are thirsty, free of charge from the Spring of Life. Come and drink before it is too late. All of this inheritance can be yours, if you would only say yes to Jesus and be a child of the Most High Father.

He gives a list of things (sins) that will never enter the Kingdom of heaven, but would be part of the second death. What amazes me is what is on the top of that list. It's cowardice, fear, and doubt that are sins (**Romans 14:23**). I have issues with folks that believe they are Christians, yet they will lock themselves in their homes or seatbelt themselves extra tight in the pews. When the Holy Spirit nudges them to say or do something and or they do not feel like it, do it anyway. It is better to do it afraid than not at all. If you believe, you do. There will be no cowards in heaven. When there is so much we need to be doing, but fear has gotten a hold of them, it's something awful. If we can go boldly into the very throne room of God (**Hebrews 4:16**), what is man compared to God? One more thing: the spirit of fear never came from God (**2 Timothy 1:7**). Our silence in this world has never been an option. Our silence is the reason why the world is in the shape it is in now. God is looking for speakers and doers of His Word.

> **Revelation 21:9-14** *"One of the seven angels who had the seven bowls full of the seven last plagues came and said to me, 'Come, I will show you the bride, the wife of the Lamb.' And he carried me away in the Spirit to a mountain great and high, and showed me the Holy City, Jerusalem, coming down out of heaven from God. It shone with the glory of God, and its brilliance was like that of a very precious jewel, like a jasper, clear as crystal. It had a great high wall with twelve gates and with twelve angels at the gates. On the gates were written the names of the twelve tribes of Israel. There were three gates on the east, three on the north, three on the south and three on the west. The wall of the city had twelve foundations, and on them were the names of the twelve apostles of the Lamb."*

The Holy City, Jerusalem continues her perfect descent towards the New Earth, soon to touch down securely in its rightful place. Moments before this gentle descent, one of the angel's wanted to show her off to John. We always want to show off our new things, whether it's a bride, a baby, a car or a home. This angel was excited and was no different, he wanted John to experience this majestic city. There is no amount of description that John could possibly muster up to justify his vision. I could not even fathom how the city shone with the glory of God. This could only be done, through a wild imaginations. I have seen several costly jewels, if you haven't, you can always search the internet or visit a local jewelry store. The only big discrepancies are that they are flawed. The most perfect stones will have their defects. Every detail and part was pure and untainted and has never been touch or made with human hands. Any place with limited or no entrance points is unwelcoming; this city has twelve gates screaming "You are Welcomed Here."

> **Revelation 21:15-27** *"The angel who talked with me had a measuring rod of gold to measure the City, its gates and its walls. The city was laid out like a square, as long as it was wide. He measured the city with the rod and found it to be 12,000 stadia in length, and as wide and high as it is long. He measured its wall and it was 144 cubits thick, by man's measurement, which the angel was using. The wall was made of jasper, and the city of pure gold, as pure as glass. The foundation of the city walls were decorated with every kind of precious stone. The first foundation was jasper, the second sapphire, the third chalcedony, the fourth emerald, the fifth sardonyx, the sixth carnelian, the seventh chrysolite, the eighth beryl, the ninth topaz, the tenth chrysoprase, the eleventh jacinth, and the twelfth amethyst. The twelve gates were twelve pearls, each gate made of a single pearl. The great street of the city was of pure gold, like transparent glass. I did not see a temple in the city, because the Lord God Almighty and the Lamb are its temple. The city does not need the sun or the moon to shine on it, for the glory of God gives it light, and the Lamb is its lamp. The nations will walk by its light, and the kings of the earth will bring their splendor into it. On no day will its gates ever be shut, for there will be no night there. The*

glory and honor of the nations will be brought into it. Nothing impure will ever enter it, nor will anyone who does what is shameful or deceitful, but only those whose names are written in the Lamb's Book of Life."

This great city is enormous. A stadia (or stadion) in ancient Greece was a typical unit of measurement. Based on the length of a sport's arena, one stadia would equal roughly 660 feet or one-eight of a mile. While some say it could be closer to 600 feet. There is a division between the theologians as some say 1500 miles (as a nice round number), others say 1363. Doing this math, I took 660 × 12,000 = 7,920,000 dividing that by 5280 feet per mile = 1,500. That would be 1500 miles high, 1500 miles wide, and 1500 miles long! There are some that believe that this City will be in the shape of an Egyptian pyramid, triangular in nature. This would seem to be false, John clearly is describing a square shape and he said so.

Doing the other math, 600 × 12,000 = 7,200,000 divide by 5280 = 1,363 would have given us 1363 miles, which is still amazing. The average cubit was 18 to 20 inches, typically the length of a human forearm. The overall thickness is between 216-240 feet or 72-80 yards, just shy in size of a football field. In this day and age, it is said that about 1200 miles upward reaches the second heaven (the first heaven is the atmosphere earth- **Psalm 104:12**, second Heaven is the stars and planets, constellations- **Isaiah 13:10**, and the third Heaven the Throne of God- **II Corinthians 12:4**). We have satellites hovering over our planet at around 800-1,000 miles away. Nothing is beyond God, it is going to be huge. We can only give this a ballpark figure, plus possible + or − for human error. The only way in or out is through the twelve gates.

Every precious stone is pure and flawless in perfected order and form. Pure gold is actually a yellowish tint and transparent as glass; unlike the metal we know on earth where we cannot see through it. With all the technology we still don't have the capabilities to refine and remove all the impurities. We are never given the shapes or sizes of these gates, only that they are made of one single giant pearl.

There will be no more arguing or fighting over different denominational churches. We will all belong to the Lord God Almighty and the Lamb of Christ temple. The sun and the moon had served   its purpose and are no longer needed. God's glory and our Lord will be our light forever. We will walk within the presence of our Creator. There will be no need to sleep for our rest, as we will be in Him. Our old bodies required sleep, it will not be necessary for our new bodies. Henceforth, there are no more nights. Even though angels will be posted at each gate, I believe they are our greeters as we come in and go out from the presence of God, since there is no need to lock the gates. There will be no more conflicts or turmoil because only glory and honor will flow throughout the nations. The only requirement is a life time membership to those whose names are in the Lamb's Book of Life. This is the description of our sinless society.

> **Revelation 22:1-6** *"The angel showed me the river of the Water of Life, as clear as crystal, flowing from the throne of God and of the Lamb down the middle of the great street of the City. On each side of the river stood the Tree of Life, bearing twelve crops of fruit, yielding its fruit every month. And the leaves of the tree are for the healing of the nations. No longer will there be any curse. The Throne of God and of the Lamb will be in the City, and His servants will serve Him. They will see His face and His name will be on their foreheads. There will be no more night. They will not need the light of the lamp or the light of the sun, for the Lord God will give them light. And they will reign forever and ever. The angel said to me, "These words are trustworthy and true. The Lord, the God of the spirits of the prophets, sent His angel to show His servants the things that must soon take place."*

The River of Life will flow from the Temple of the Son and the Father to the community, in the middle of this big City, the water is as clear as crystal. There will be no pollutants on top, around or underneath dead or alive, nor algae or fungus. The Tree of Life will be planted between the River of Life. It will bear twelve different fruits per year, one for each month. In the New Heaven and New Earth, man will be divided into two classes, kings and citizens, just like it will be in the millennium. It will differentiate between "people" in verse **21:3** and "son" in verse **21:7**. The sons will dwell in the city, they are the glorified saints throughout the ages. They will have a spiritual body. But the "nations" and the "peoples" will still have fleshly bodies. They will be the ones transferred from the millennium. There will still be the fleshly bodies, but there will be no death, sickness, or diseases.

Since there is the fleshly body, there will inevitably be weaknesses, even though there will be no sickness and death. The leaves of the Tree of Life are for "the Healing of the nations." The physical flesh bodies will have limitations where the Spiritual bodies won't. By eating the leaves, they will forever be strong on the New Earth. For the overcoming believers, they will not eat of the leaves, but of the fruits. There will not be any curses looming over us, such as generational or cycle curses. We will forever see God, which was His plan and desire from the beginning (relationship communion), and we will carry His New Name. Because of God's genuine love for His creation, He saw that it was good. He has sent messengers so that none would perish. Are we hearing, listening and heeding the Living Words of truth?

> **Revelation 22:7-11** *"Behold, I Am coming soon! Blessed is he who keeps the words of the prophecy in this book. I, John, am the one who heard and saw these things. And when I had heard and seen them, I fell down to worship at the feet of the angel who had been showing them to me. But he said to me, 'Do not do it! I am a fellow servant with you and with your brothers the prophets and of all who keep the words of this book. Worship God!' Then he told me, 'Do not seal up the words of the prophecy of this book, because the Time is Near. Let him who does wrong continue to do wrong; let him who is vile continue to be vile; let him who does right continue to do right; and let him who is holy continue to be holy.'"*

King Jesus explains three times in these next three sections that He is Coming Soon. He is stressing the point as a hope for the believers and a warning to the unbelievers. We must continue to keep our house in order and stay the course to witness in our every day life.

All of the Old Testament prophets would refer to the End Time events in terms of the "Latter Days," now it has become more personal and closer. John in the first century entered the stage of the End Times. He writes the words that he was given, as if His return was just around the corner, even in his days. John was the last major prophet and key eye witness to what will be unfolding in our Last Days. He was so shocked and amazed over all that he had seen, that he tried to worship the angel. But the angel refused and forbid him to do so. The angel made it clear to worship only God alone, not our spouses, our jobs, money, our hobbies, things, or demons. In Daniel, he was told to seal up this portion of his prophecy, until the Time of the End. John is not told to do such a thing, because the Time is Nearer. So since the first century and to our present we have been in the Time is Near era. The last sentence is very important, so many people beat themselves up trying to force other to make what we feel are the best choices for them. That is not our job or our purpose for the Kingdom of heaven. It is the Holy Spirit alone that motivates and convicts, we are only the messengers and witnesses. We are to give them the information and let them decide for themselves. We are also only responsible for ourselves. Face it, people will do wrong and people will do right, and everything in between, it is their freedom to choose.

> **Revelation 22:12-17** *"Behold, I Am coming soon! My reward is with Me, and I will give to everyone according to what he has done. I Am the Alpha and Omega, the First and the Last, the Beginning and the End. Blessed are those who wash their robes, that they may have the right to the Tree of Life and may go through the gates into the City. Outside are the dogs, those who practice magic arts, the sexually immoral, the murderers, the idolaters and everyone who loves and practices falsehood. I, Jesus, have sent My angel to give you this testimony for the Churches. I Am the Root and the Offspring (see* **chapter 12***) of David, and the bright Morning Star." The Spirit and the bride say, "Come!" And let him who hears say, "Come!" Whoever is thirsty, let him come; and whoever wishes, let him take the free gift of the Water of Life."*

Our Lord Jesus is our great Rewarder and He will reward us according to the things we have done, while on earth. Or the things we were supposed to do and did not. Other translations refers to "those who wash their robes," to those who keep His commandments or are partakers of His righteousness, as one and the same. We no longer live but have died to ourselves and are alive in Christ when we were born again. We will have free access through the gates of New Jerusalem and to the Tree of Life.

Outsiders, those that are not allowed within the City's gates are the dogs, this is a picture of the evil wickedness in immoral thoughts and deeds. The falsehood can be as small as half-truths or little white lies, deception will not be a part of this community nor will these things enter into the gates. Jesus Himself sent His messengers to give John this personal testimony for the Churches (the Gentiles, Israelites, adopted, and offspring). Even though the book of Revelation as a whole was written at first for the Seven Churches (the church age), it is also believed to go out to whoever has Spiritual ears to hear. It stopped after chapter three and started focusing foremost on God's creation. He was a descendant from David of the tribe of Judah. The True Spirit has always referred to the Trinity of the Godhead and the bride has always referred to the Church (the true believers). Jesus Himself is beckoning the lost to Come, whoever thirsts to drink from the Well of Living Water. It is a free gift all you have to do is receive it.

> **Revelation 22:18-21** *"I warn everyone who hears the words of the prophecy of this book: If anyone adds anything to them, God will add to him the plagues described in this book. And if anyone takes words away from this book of prophecy, God will take away from him his share in the Tree of life and in the Holy City, which are described in this book. He who testifies to these things says, 'Yes, I Am coming soon.' Amen. Come, Lord Jesus. The grace of the Lord Jesus be with God's people. Amen."*

The book of Revelation ends with two warning: the first, if anyone adds anything to this book God will add to their punishments described within it. And the second, if anyone subtracts anything from this book God will take away their rewards in eternity. We are only to speak the *Truth,* no more no less. Jesus Christ is coming soon. So be it.

My only hope and desire is to shed some light on these signs and the possibilities of the things going on in the world around us. It was never to confuse you, the reader. There is no doubt our Lord Jesus Christ is coming very soon. Some may say He is literally just around the corner.

But I say He is a lot closer than one might think. He is knocking at the door if anyone opens that door He will come in and sup with you. May God our Father Creator of all things and through His Grace, Mercy and love Richly Bless you.

CHAPTER TEN

NEW WORLD GOVERNMENT RISING

THE DEFINITION OF Globalization is the process of moving from a Nation State to a Global Governance or government. This will only happen through careful and methodically planned stages. It will not just happen overnight. It is not about the overall big picture. That will happen soon enough! It is about working all the smaller puzzle pieces together and how it will eventually form and be completed. Be aware of what has been going on throughout our history, including up to our present time.

Our world is in dangerous times. I have noticed several "red flags." So how did we get to this point and where are we going from here? The Bible refers to this as the Cup of God's Wrath or Dread. It has been quickly filling and once it starts to overflow, then God's Wrath will follow.

In case you are not aware, lawlessness has been increasing within this last century or so. Now it has gotten so out of control, with crazy evil and selfish thinking.

Vladimir Lenin (1870-1924), former Soviet Union Premier once said, "A lie told often enough becomes the truth." Morality is slowly becoming a thing of the past and immorality the new, improved norm or way of doing things.

I will share some nuggets that you can follow to verify on your own. We learn best when we do our own work or studies (research). This is Not a history book! As we continue to push God out of our society, do note He will be replaced with something else and that is Not a good thing.

Keep in mind that God is Good **(Psalm 107:1; James 1:17)** and God is Just **(Isaiah 30:18; Ephesians 6:9)**. So God is Never mean or evil when He poured out His Wrath. We need to know all the characteristics of God, for example He "is" also truth **(Psalm 119:60; Hebrews 6:18; Titus 1:2; & I John 5:20)**. There are two clear examples of God's Wrath, after He gave mankind every chance to humble and repent. During the days of Noah **(Genesis 6:5-8)**, this generation became very wicked and abominable. And during the days of Lot **(Genesis 18:20-21; 19:23-25)**, this generation was very evil and perverted. We are in the very mist of a very cold, selfish, and callous generation **(Hosea 4:1-3; II Timothy 3:1-5; & I Peter 3:20)**.

In this chapter I will briefly discuss and cover parts of America's beginnings, even before we became the United States and how we got to where we are. Believe me, all of the things that are going on today did not just happen within these last few years or decades, it was escalated. I will be as brief as I can and move on.

One of the very first things the Pilgrims did was started an educational system in the New World. The only book(s) that was used was the Geneva Bible. Most of them were known as Puritans, they started the school system putting God first in the 1600's. Prior to this, was the Dark Ages and the Bibles were very scarce, only reserved for the Clergies. There was also no such thing as educational learning at that time. It was vitally important for them to teach the next generation not to be ignorant, but to live a moral life style through the principles of the Bible.

By 1690 the New England Primer was first published and added as a scriptural teaching tool and was used in conjunction with Biblical teachings. It was last printed in 1843 and discontinued circulation years later. By this time other books were being added while the Bible slowly got pushed further and further down on the shelves.

So, where were these schools located or did they build school-houses? They were first placed within the walls of the churches. They had church services during the weekend and school during the week, a win-win situation. When we started to divide between the two (late 1800's), things started to become more and more secular (a problem). Since then we have continued to push God out.

What about the Salem Witch trials in 1692-1693? This was one of our many dark times in American history. It started and quickly stopped and in the end only nineteen were unjustly condemned and murdered. We have learned from our past and the horrible wrong that was done. Most of them if not were tortured and beaten into confessing. We used this example within our legal system today; "Innocent until proven Guilty," Not the other way around. We are also not allowed to physically beat or abuse anyone into confessing or submission.

During this same era (1500's-1600's), Europe had their own witch trials, that murdered over one hundred thousand people within a span of about two centuries. Most of them were from the poor communities, the outcasts, the sick, and mentally challenged. Others became a threat and were challenging the government run churches. We did pick-up a lot of bad habits from the country we originally came from.

Next on the list is slavery, which has almost been around since the beginning of time. There is a big difference between being a slave and being a servant. Even though they both can be used interchangeably, the same thing with a demon and a fallen angel.

During Abraham's life time there were servants forming in society. The first recorded term for slaves, was round about 2000 B.C., when the Israelites became slaves in Egypt under harsh working conditions. They did not start off as slaves.

Being a slave has nothing to do with one's skin color or pigmentation. It is not a black or white thing. In fact we also had Indian and Asian slaves in America in the 1800's, we do not hear much if anything about that. Granted this had a lot to do with the African trade ships. The slave trade may have gotten its start in 1619, but it began well before this, in the later 1500's. Most of them came through the southern ports, where cheap labor was needed for farming. I heard there was one ship prior to 1619 (earlier in the 1600's), that landed in a northern port, only to get kicked back out to sea, because the northerners were highly against selling other human beings as slaves. Also during this time period between 1400's-1700's they had something called "indentured servants." This was also something that was going on during Biblical times to pay off a person's debt, it was not a new thing. It was for those who could not pay or afford the cost to travel to the New World. There would be an agreement between the two parties. One would pay their way while the other agreed to serve them. It was usually for a six year period. There were some that did not want to give them their freedom per contract, because they liked the idea of having a personal servant waiting on them. They ended up being forced into a lifetime of slavery. Today we would call this sex or human trafficking.

The last point here is the fact that there were actually more 'black slave owners" than white slave owners. In the US Census in 1830 there were 3,775 free blacks who owned 12,740 black slaves. In Louisiana 965 free blacks owned 4,206 slaves. In South Carolina 464 free blacks owned 2,715 slaves. This (slavery) did not happen in the north. Notice this is in the southern parts.

We had a mental divide starting within America way before the Civil War. The folks in the north were very much highly against slavery and were known as "Abolitionists."

The three-fifths clause or rule that applied to the Black Americans, unfortunately was justifiable because the southerners wanted to count all of their slaves, which would add more seats and votes in Congress. Yet they were not allowed to vote, because they were considered property. So this was done to prevent this sickness from spreading.

During this time period God was very active and very much a part in all four main areas in society; the *homes*, the *schools*, the *churches*, and the *government*. Today we would consider it lucky if God was in at least one of these.

Most of our founding fathers believed that we were all created equal. Most of them founded or were active members of several American Bible Societies and churches during that time. In addition many of them were also missionaries to the Native Americans. They were *Not* Deist or Agnostic, most of them did in fact believed in the "One true God." The common name they used for God during that time was "Providence." This was because at that time the only Biblical translation they had was the Geneva Bible. This Bible uses one of the titles for God as, Providence, 144 times. So this was not some secular deist or agnostic slang, as some history professors teach.

The blacks and whites both fought side by side during the Revolution War. So it was not a white man's war. There were also at least ten Black Americans in Congress back in the early 1800's, which was huge since we were a small underdog, growing country.

The famous Jefferson Bibles, many people do not understand his reasoning or whys behind them. The first one, *The Philosophy of Jesus of Nazareth,* was completed in 1804, but no known copies exist today. The second one, *The Life and Morals of Jesus of Nazareth,* was completed in 1820. He put them together as a witnessing and missionary tool for the Native Americans. He was basically saying, it is all about Jesus and nothing else matters.

Now many believe because of this and that he owned a Koran book, that he was a Deist or an Atheist. No, he was a Christian. He was also dealing with the Tripoli pirates, which happened to be Muslim. Know your enemies as thyself.

A French political scientist and historian Alexis de Tocqueville was the first writer to describe this (new) country as "exceptional" following his travels here in 1831. We still had our battles against evil, yes we were not perfect. But we were still known to be a uniquely different country, unknown to the known world at the time.

What about the "Great Awakening"? Now first, God does not just do things for the sake of just doing things. There are always reasons why and there is always a cost. In the first century there was a great persecution. This happened as a result of the "Great Out Pouring" and this lasted over a century.

The First Great Awakening lasted from the middle of the 1730's to the early 1770's, about three decades; what followed was the Revolutionary War (1775-1783). The Second Great Awakening lasted from the late 1790's to the late 1840's, about five decades; what followed was the War of 1812 (1812-1815) and the Civil War (1861-

1865). The Third Great Awakening lasted from the early 1890's to the late 1930's, about five decades; what followed was the Spanish and American War (1898), WWI (1914-1918), WWII (1939-1945) & Korean War (1950-1953). The Fourth Great Awakening (controversial) lasted from the early 1960's to the late 1970's, about one decade; what followed was an American Social Revolution; Civil Rights, gay rights, hippy (make love not war) movements (drugs, orgies, and war protest), Vietnam War era (1959-1975). You will need to research on your own the ongoing battles during and shortly after these time periods. They were all far more than just a quaint little revival. The next and last Great Awakening will be happening very soon.

Separation of Church and State is a well-known phrase. However, it is not found anywhere in the Constitution of the United States. This all started because Thomas Jefferson quoted the originator of this phrase, Roger Williams (1603-1683) "a great (high) wall of separation between church and state", in a personal letter, between him and the Danbury Baptist Association in 1802. This same letter was used in a Supreme Court case in 1947 *Everson v. Board of Education.*

Separation of Church and State simply means that the government cannot exercise its authority in establishing a National Religion or a State Denomination. We should be able to come together regardless of what your church affiliation is. Schools constitute a local extension of the government which cannot make religion mandatory for all students. This clause of the First Amendment is the "Establishment Clause." This means that schools cannot have assemblies which promote or force a religion. And classroom teachers cannot promote one religion (or non-religion such as atheism) over another. The Establishment Clause limits the free speech rights of teachers, principals and staff when communicating with students in schools. This term has been misinterpreted over the years.

Our Founding Fathers never meant to separate State and Church, but instead just wanted to make sure that the government does not interfere with religion. Basically telling the government, hands off in regards to this subject. Especially, that it does not officially establish one particular religion or denomination over another or establish non-religion over religion. It was always about Freedom of Religion not Freedom from Religion. It was to be able to worship, "The" God your way not the government's way. This was to worship the One and only true God, not just a or any gods. The First Amendment states in the Establishment Clause: CONGRESS SHALL MAKE NO LAW RESPECTING AN ESTABLISHMENT OF RELIGION, OR PROHIBITING THE FREE EXERCISE THEREOF…"

After the 13th and 14th Amendments were ratified in 1865 and 1868, it made way for a special kind of evil, the establishment in 1865 of the Ku Klux Klan, and personal attacks on the Black American. Some of these members were also church members. Today it has gotten so bad that when anyone who disagree with a particular group of people, they are considered white supremacists, terrorist or hate groups (guilt by association); which are the same used for the KKK.

At the turn of the twentieth century our country tried to bring the world together by spearheading what was called the League of Nations, a vision led by former President Woodrow Wilson (1913-1921). There were talks about starting this League of Nations during WW1. After WW1 ended (1914-1918) with over eight million deaths, reality started settling in and shocked the world. No other war in history came close to that many fatalities. It was finally founded in 1920, but did not last. It quickly started fizzling away by the 1930's, and then eventually failed and dissolve after about twenty-five short years in the mid 1940's. It was just hanging in the balance, by threads, before it eventually fell apart.

The failure came about because of the fear of a nation to give up their sovereignty. The United States never join the League of Nations because of this simple fact. The world was just not ready for this big step, yet the hunger and the desire was still lingering. So the United States did not really support this League of Nation's vision that then President Wilson had. Other countries shared in that same view point. At that point there just were not enough key financial players or big hitters that believed in a United League of Nations. The ones that did join really had nothing to lose.

A little background information about President Woodrow Wilson. Most of us have some forms of skeletons in our closets. First, I would like to say that the man was very smart. His former job was as a president of Princeton University; he was known as an educator. He wrote and published a five volume book set, about our American history. This has done more damage to our Country, causing a huge division between the black Americans and the white Americans. The black Americans along with the white Americans played a huge part in the Revolutionary War. Not so in these books. He erased the black Americans out of that time in history and depicted the black Americans through pictures as monsters, missing links, or as ape men. He also believed in the Confederation mind set verses the Union. He was also a known member of the Ku Klux Klan.

Now we all have strengths and weaknesses. He did get us out of WWI, he was a strong advocate in reforming the child labor laws, as well as working through the reconstruction and industrial evolution eras.

The reality eventual hit home after WWII's death counts which shocked the world, with over 52 million deaths in six years.

In the 1920's an educator and psychologist by the name of John Dewey (1859-1952) and his group of cohorts changed our educational system to what we have today. Prior to the 1920's the highest grade level to complete was the Eight grade. There was no such thing as a High School grade level (9th through 12th). One of his famous quote was, "There ain't no God, there ain't no Soul." His philosophy was "we no longer want you (the students) to think for yourself, we will think for you just do what we say or tell you." The testing was also changed to introduce new testing curriculum such as: True & False, Multiple choice, and fill in the blank questions. Prior to all this, their testing were based solely on Essays and Debates. When they all graduated from school, they took the college entrance exams by the ripe old age of 12, some as early as ten. They had their college Degrees by the time they were sixteen or seventeen years old from Universities such as Yale, Harvard, or Princeton and went on to become doctors and lawyers.

Since then, we have not been even close to challenging the next generation. No offense, but there are a whole lot of adults that are as dumb as rocks. I have personally met some of them. Some of them are very nice people, they just do not know how to think for themselves. It is really kind of sad they do not know how to handle life's problems.

We once held the educational Bar high, now it is but only ankle high if even that.

But to be fair, there was an industrial revolution still going on at the time. The workforce did not want a bunch of thinkers and debaters. They only wanted a bunch of doers and followers. This did a lot of damage towards our educational system and the future of our country. Now we have a lot of folks in our government, about 80 percent that have no clue regarding any of our founding documents, such as The Constitution or The Declaration of Independence.

In 1935 the United States made changes to the one dollar bills. Since that time, our one dollar bills have had on the back the words, "NOVUS ORDO SECLORUM." This is located inside the ribbon just under the pyramid on the backside. These words are Latin for "New World Order" or Time of Ages. It was also former President Franklin D. Roosevelt's (1933-45) driving force and vision for a one world government as well.

In addition to a few public programs he implemented to assist those in need during the "Great Depression"… PERIOD, not to last for some eighty years plus later. It is Not the government's job or responsibility to pick-up these pieces. Though they are responsible to fix the oppressive state they purposely caused on their people. Only then it is supposed to be the churches place to do that. The founders original intent was for the government to stay "thin and limited" not fat and out of shape. They were "all" supposed to have been temporary assistance.

Former President Harry S. Truman (1945-53) carried out this dream and helped to establish the United Nations in 1945. These countries were now allowed to join without having to give up their total sovereignty… yet.

In recent years the Council on Foreign Relations (CFR) has instituted a program called the International Institution and Global Governance (IIGG). Its role is to assess existing regional and global government mechanisms such as over-population problems, global warming, terrorism and economic melt-downs.

Rear Admiral Chester Ward said, "The most powerful clique in these elite groups have one objective in common, they want to bring about the surrender of the sovereignty and the national independence of the United States. A second clique of international members of the CFR comprises of the Wall Street international bankers and their key agents. Primarily, they want the world banking monopoly, from whatever power to end up in the control of the global government."

CFR and IIGG program—The Re-Conceptualizing National Sovereignty, Board of Director during one of their meetings (name unknown) said, "Among the most important factors determining the future of global governance will be the attitude of the United States." For now, the Constitution stands in the way. Very few countries have been as sensitive to the restrictions on their freedom of action or as jealous in guarding their sovereignty prerogatives. The new international obligations, according to director of the IIGG Stewart M. Patrick, "Seek to turn the page on what many perceived to be 'a cowboy unilateralism' of the Bush years, by embracing multilateral cooperation, rekindling U.S. alliances and partnerships and engaging in sustain diplomacy within the U.N. framework."

Pope Francis is believed to be the last and final Pope, prior to the End of the Age. This same Pope gave the Medallion of Peace to Mahmoral Abbas, Palestinian President, stating, "…destroying the bad spirit of war… claims it was appropriate because you (Abbas) are an angel of peace." The same individual is known as one of the leaders of Hamas, which stands for deception and supports warring against Israel and God.

In 2013 Pope Francis gave the Highest Order of the Star of Honor, awarded to Nayef Hawatmeh a known Palestinian terrorist that has attacked school children and teachers. To date he has killed 22 school children and four teachers after taking them hostage in Ma'a lot. He also killed nine children and three adults in an attack on a school bus. In addition he killed seven in a Jerusalem bombing and killed four hostages in an apartment building in Beit Sheam.

Pope Francis blames ISIS on fundamentalism and was quoted in saying, "We have our share of them. All religions have these little groups… fundamentalist are Christians that believe the Bible as true (the Book of Life), likewise Muslims believe the Koran to be true (the book of war). (Islamic leader Abu Bakr Al-Baghdadi said, "Islam was never a religion of peace, but Islam is the religion of fighting.")

Our sovereignty is currently hanging in the balance. The last three Presidents; Clinton, Bush, and Obama have all gone through the United Nations to declare war and totally bypassed our Constitution and Congress, which states that only Congress can authorize war.

Our government was created so that *no* one person can ever have total authority or power, this is called the "Power (or balance) of the Purse." Congress is the one that makes the laws, not the president.

The president does have Veto power. The Supreme Court Justices are supposed to interprets these laws according to the Constitution. There are several possible laws if signed will weaken our country's sovereignty. The most recent debate concerns gun control, or to ban guns altogether country wide. This alone will destroy our Second Amendment "rights" and will cause illegal searches and void the rights of individuals to protect themselves. Other debates examples are, the Green New Deal, Freedom of Speech to oppress the truths and calling it miss or disinformation, the famous WOKE-ism, Cancel Culture, and Critical Race Theory. Now there are also arguments around the recent overturn of Roe v Wade, abortion issues.

I was overly concern with what I knew about Barak Obama. There have been a lot of red flags during his administration. I choose not to share any of these concerns, unless I end up going down a rabbit hole. Some examples to research would be the IRS Scandals (Tea Party), the apology tour, pro-abortion and an active stance within the gay community, the Iran funding of 400 billion dollars, catch and release policy, chain migration policy, and the weakening of our military and the economy to mention a few.

Note that he has done the most damage during his eight years in office than any other past president. Though President Biden has now quickly surpassed him in his first term alone, I did not think it could have gotten any worse. Wide open southern boarder is not healthy for our Country. Biden has single handedly destroyed all of what President Trump has accomplished, such as a strong economy (jobs and cost of living) stronger military, progress towards a strong and secure southern wall, independence from other counties, and

America respected internationally. In addition to making all the UN counties pay their own fair and equal share. Prior to this the United States picked up these bills that they were supposed to have paid.

For the last few decades one particular party has been trying to attack and destroy our God given rights, which this country was truly founded on. And to try to rewrite the Constitution, mainly the first and second amendments of our Bill of Right, others will follow. We have all the authority and power given to us by God, to change the direction this country is heading.

For the last few decades, there also seems to be a great confusion regarding ones gender. That just sounds crazy if one cannot figure out the difference. And these are so called professionals that are having problems explaining these things for fear of offending someone's feelings. Along with all this follows massive sex change surgeries and out of control sexual assaults and sexual perversion. This sounds a lot to me like the days of Noah and Lot in our day (**Genesis 6 & 19**). In addition to this mankind's hearts will continue to grow selfish and colder (**Matthew 24:12**).

There will always be a conflict between good and evil. You have a choice to make. Which side will you fight for? You cannot stay neutral, that is why we are where we are… we did nothing to prevent it. It is high time we wake up and take back our marriages, our families, our communities, our schools, our churches, and Yes our country.

The time lines within the last 155 years (1865-2020):

1869-1871–The panic and depression of the stock market fall.

1870-1871–Franco-German War only lasted about ten months, Germany's victory and France's loss. This marked the beginning rise of the first Reich of the Leopard's head (Germany). This is were the feathers of the fowl was removed from the leopard in Daniel's vision; as France's national emblem is the Rooster.

1893–The first Parliament of the world religious leaders was established and the 100th anniversary was held in Chicago. Robert

Mueller former director of the Federal Bureau of Investigation said at the 2000th United Religious Conference, "We have a need for a unified religious leader."

1901-1904—The panic and depression of the stock market fall.

1913—The Federal Reserve Bank was established, signed and ratified into law by President Howard Taft (1909-1913). Paul Warburg and about six others met in secret on Jekyll Island in 1910 to form the ground work which later became the Federal Reserve. This was all completed during the House and Senate's holiday (Christmas) shutdown.

1914-1940's—The first time the phrase "Open Door Policy" is used, by President Woodrow Wilson (1913-1921) in 1914. This "Open Door Policy" meant free trade and commerce for big industries, benefiting ownerships, forcing small and weak counties to confide with colonizing through slave laborers and poor conditions.

1914-1918—WWI: Serbian nationalist Gavrilo Princip assassinated Archduke Franz Ferdinand and his wife in Sarajevo, sparking the outbreak of the war. The second Reich, rise and fall of the Leopard's head of Germany with 8.2 million deaths.

1916—The Brookings Institution was established as a private organization (think tank) devoted to studying public government policies and issues.

1917-1923—Bolshevik Revolution started and became a Russian Revolution turned Civil War, an unrest between the government and the people. After the bloody massacres they soon became a new political party, Communist. The immigrant Jewish people were forced to flee the Soviet Union.

1919–The Treaty of Versailles, the WWI peace treaty agreement with Germany and the rest of the world. Germany violated this Treaty and ended up being a huge failure, since WWII broke out.

1919-1946–The League of Nations started forming in 1919 and was established in 1920. It was later officially disbanded in 1946, due to the lack of funding and key powerful countries. All of their members were small and poorer counties. The United States government voted down becoming a member due to surrendering our sovereignty.

1921–The Council on Foreign Relations most key political players (cabinet members), became a part of presidential administrations, regardless of political affiliation. This is not a governmental agency, but a private institution. Their mission statement: An independent, nonpartisan membership organization and publisher dedicated to helping its members better understand the world and the foreign policy choices facing the United States and other countries.

1929-1939–The stock market crashes, followed by the "Great Depression."

1934-1938–Establishments of government programs such as food stamps, Medicare, Medicaid, public works and assistance. The forming of the first nation wide individual identification card, Social Security Card.

1939-1945–WWII, the third Reich rise and fall of the Leopard's head of Germany (52 million deaths).

1941–(December 7th) The United States declares war and enters WWII, when Japan attacked the United States at Pearl Harbor, Hawaii. Twenty-one ships lost or damaged with 1,993 dead.

1942–Planned Parenthood was founded by atheist Margret Sanger. Its purpose was to murder innocent (minority) babies through abortions. This did not become legal in the United Sates until years later in 1973. It quickly became an international corporation in the years following.

1944–The creation of the International Monetary Fund (IMF) an economic structure for a world banking system.

1945–United Nations was founded. It was President Franklin D. Roosevelt's vision; but it was President Harry S. Truman that helped make it come to pass.

1948–(May 14th) Israel becomes a nation in a single day, fulfilling an Old Testament prophecy (**Isaiah 66:8**).

1950–Introduction of the barcode system, required on all manufacturing products.

1950-1953–The Korean War, known as the forgotten war, with 5 million deaths, mainly civilian causalities, with Russia fighting with the North Korean's (Communist party) and the United States fighting with the South Korean's (Democratic party). It ended in a stalemate and a divided country.

1954–(Lyndon B.) Johnson Amendment, a provision in the US tax code that prohibits all non-profit organizations (targeted at churches) from endorsing or opposing political candidates. In 2017, President Trump repealed this provision, arguing it violated freedom of speech rights.

1955-1957–Dwight D. Eisenhower required the motto, "In God We Trust" on all coin (1955) and paper currency (1957).

1957–The Treaty of Rome aka (the European) Common Market created.

1955-1975–Vietnam War, in 1959 we entered a war we should not have been in. More than 3 million people (including over 58,000 Americans) were killed in the Vietnam War, and more than half of the dead were Vietnamese civilians. This was another war between Russia and the United States, trying to keep communism from spreading. Our last troops left that country in 1973. Of all veterans, Vietnam veterans suffered the highest rate of post-traumatic stress, divorces, suicides, alcoholism, and drug addictions.

1960's–(Social Revolution decade); civil rights movement, woman's liberation, gay rights, abortion rights, war on poverty, war protest. Assassinations of John F. Kennedy, Martin Luther King Jr. and Robert F. Kennedy.

1960–Madeline Murray O'Hair, an Atheist fought and won legally in removing Bible reading and prayers in public schools. As the years progress, it slowly disappeared from our educational system.

1961–The Berlin Wall is erected, separating the East (communism) from the West German (democratic) side. Possibly one of the heads of the Leopard that was wounded.

1961–Also the Bay of Pigs, a botched up invasion between Cuban exiles and the United States.

1962–Cuban Missile Crisis, 13 days on the brink of a nuclear war between the United States and the Soviet Union.

1967–Israel's "Six Day" war, a victory against all odds that granted Israel twice the original land mass.

1970's–The Trilateral Commission was founded, headed by Jimmy Carter. A different name for meaning the same thing—Council on Foreign Relations.

1973–The Paris Peace Accord was signed to end the Vietnam War, another violation and failure, within two years the country was turned over to communism.

1973–Yom Kippur War (Day of Atonement), against all odds, Israel was attack by most of their neighboring counties. Both sides suffered losses.

1973–Roe vs Wade, Supreme Court legalizes abortions. Over 100 million babies murdered since and counting.

1976–Freedom from Religion Foundation; an non-profit organization, which advocates for Atheists, Agnostics, and non-theists. Challenges the legitimacy of many Federal and State programs that are Faith-Based.

1982–Camp David Accord was a horrible peace talks where Israel lost most of their land that was gained from Six Day war.

1989–The Fall of the Berlin Wall, possibly the healing of the wounded Leopard head. This could possibly be the start or birth of the New World Order making possible Globalization.

1990-1991–Gulf War, Iraq invasion of Kuwait (Desert Shield/ Desert Storm).

1992–The forming of the European Union (EU) a political structure, presently has twenty-seven member nations. The Maastrichi Treaty which gave each nation's power and control to the 27 non-elected appointed individuals. Green Cross and the Earth Summit were organized as environmentalist, interlocking laws around air and water, climate change, and global warming.

1994–The North American Free Trade Association (NAFTA) agreements, later was changed to the World Trade Organization

(WTO). During the same year Asia Pacific Economic Cooperation (APEC) was also founded.

1997–The Kyoto Treaty climate and economic laws. As of 2009, 181 nations out of 192 signed this making it the supreme law of the land. Then President George W. Bush refused to sign, saying it would have surrendered our sovereignty rights as a nation to a world community.

1998–The United Nations adopted an International (world) Criminal Court system.

1999–The Euro, the first common currency established in the European Union.

2000–The Global Summit:"Responsibility to Protect", Signed in 2005 by 153 nations, it gave the United Nations authority to over throw hostile governments.

2001–Terrorist attack on the World Trade Centers and the Pentagon which left 2,996 murdered, possibly the start of WWIII.

2002–The establishment of the African Union.

2003-2021–Invasion in Iraq and Afghanistan; a war against Taliban and ISIS terrorist.

2009–Lisbon Treaty established European executive commission given voting rights and to make choices behind closed doors, taking the citizen's rights away from them. The Parliament no longer had any authority. The birth of the "New Revised Holy Roman Empire." European Union adopted its own Constitution.

2016–Underdog Donald Trump won the Presidential Election against Hillary Rodham Clinton, which shocked the country. He did more to stabilize and improve the country than any other recent administration. Trump spent most of his term fighting the lies and corruption. We gained a stronger economy, became more energy independent and increased jobs (keystone pipe and southern wall). The cost of living was down. Life in general was good. He also removed the catch and release policy and chain of migration policy from the previous administration, which were both bad.

2019-2020 COVID Pandemic, rioting, looting, and unrest across America. The pandemic came out of a lab in China and quickly went around the globe. It has been reported that the (World Health Organization) W.H.O. knew about this and did nothing to prevent the spread. A quick response from President Trump helped to minimize the spread. Fear swept through the country. I see a possible new annual vaccination shot, similar to the yearly flu shots and childhood booster shots.

Rioting and looting as small businesses burned to the ground. Robberies and murders spread to the streets. In other parts of the country they were calling it the "Summer of Love" and demanding for Defunding the Police. Meanwhile the Black Lives Matter (BLM movement) came about that had nothing to do with any lives let alone black lives. That was a scam that fed off of people's emotions to support their corrupt organization.

2020–Election fraud: The first time in U.S history where any one party stole an election. It should have been a huge landside for the then Republican President Donald Trump, but instead went to the then Democratic candidate Joseph Biden and his Build Back Better policy. All while Biden hid mostly in his basement, as Trump had large turnout rallies. The corruption was huge, not just in the Federal Government, but also within other branches of departments and agencies as well. Even through the State Governments and the legal system, including Judges, District Attorneys, and lawyers. President Biden single handedly destroyed the good Trump accomplished. He seems to be a puppet; his health had been declining rapidly before his presidential run. Our country is in very bad shape and continues to fall apart, with the high cost of living, food shortage, increase gas and oil prices. His approval rating is the lowest of any president, at 34 percent.

2021–President Biden withdraws all military forces from the Mideast. There was no planning and they left many allies behind, as ISIS terrorist quickly took control.

Famous quotes:

Norman Thomas–(1884-1968) US Socialist Presidential Candidate from 1928-1948: "The American people will never knowingly adopt Socialism. But under the name of Liberalism they will adopt every fragment of the Socialist program until one day America will be a Socialist nation, without knowing how it happened."

William Benton–(1900-1973) Assistant Secretary of State (1946): "As long as a child breathes the poisoned air of nationalism, education in World-mindedness can procure only precarious results. As we have pointed out, it is frequently the family that infects the child with extreme nationalism. The schools should therefore combat family attitudes that favor nationalism. We shall see presently recognized in nationalism the major obstacle to the development of World-mindedness. We are at the beginning of a long process of breaking down the walls of national sovereignty UNESCO (United Nations Educational Scientific and Cultural Organization) must be the pioneer."

James Paul Warburg–(1896-1969) Banker (son of Paul Warburg) in 1950 before the US Senate committee on Foreign Relations: "We will have a World Government whether you like it or not. The only question is whether that government will be achieved by conquest or consent."

Pope Pius XII–(1876-1958) in December of 1960, Catholic Lawyer Robert F. Drinan wrote about the Pope in the "Legacy to World Federalism". 1. The reaffirmation of the necessity of a super national world order. 2. Accepting the United Nations but with ceaseless efforts to strengthen it. 3. Promote the fullest cooperation with every agency that promotes international friendship. (Pius was unabashed internationalist believed in globalization). He desired and sought and prayed for a future world political organization tuned to the spirit of federalism. "…Catholics… above all…must realize that they are called to overcome every vestige of nationalistic narrow mindedness." "Catholics have the obligation of insisting on the ratification of the genocide pact."

Pope John XXIII–(1881-1963) in July 1963, written about what the Pope believed in the General Resolution, along with its plea to the United Nations "to become more equal to the magnitude and mobility of its tasks," the Pope's encyclical made a case for the establishment of world government with all the cogency of his theologians best proofs that God exists. In Vatican language Pacern en terries calls world government a "public authority" but defines it as "having worldwide power and endowed with the proper means for the efficacious pursuit of the universal common good." The Pope held that such a government must be founded because all nations are now interdependent.

Bishop Pierre Boillon of France–(1911-1996) October 1965: "Therefore we must emphasize the great moral responsibility to empower an international authority to prevent war. The entire world must become aware that if this institution is to become effective, every nation must renounce its ultimate sovereignty to this universal authority. This is an obligation. If nations, if rulers of nations, if public opinion will not accept this renunciation, then they really are voting for war, however beautiful may be their speeches on peace."

Pope Paul VI–(1897-1978) March 1967: "Who can fail to see the need and importance of thus gradually coming to the establishment of a world authority capable of taking effective actions on the juridical and political planes? Delegates to international organizations, public officials, gentlemen of the press, and teachers and educators—all of you must realize that you have your part to play in the construction of a New World Order."

Richard Gardner–(1927-2019) Former Deputy Assistant of State in 1974 Foreign Affairs magazine,: "We are likely to do better by building our house of World Order from the bottom up rather than from the top down... an end run around national sovereignty eroding it piece by piece, is likely to get us to World Order faster than the old fashioned assault."

Mikhail Gorbachev–(1931-2022) Former Soviet Union Prime Minister, in 1987: "We are moving toward a new World Order, and the world of communism. We shall never turn off that road."

Strobe Talbott–(1946-) Deputy Secretary of State during the Clinton administration, president of the Brookings Institution in 2000. In 1992 he said, "In the twenty-first century national sovereignty would cease to exist; that we would all answer to a single global authority."

David Rockefeller–(1915-2017) President of Chase Manhattan Bank, President of the Council on Foreign Relations and Founder and President of the Trilateral Commission; in a statement to the United Nations in 1994: "We are on the verge of a global transformation. All we need is the right major crisis and the nations will accept the New World Order."

President W.J. Clinton–(1946-) To the United Nations assembly in 1997; "I believe it is time to establish a one world court system." (came to pass in 1998 and in 2009 has issued its first arrest warrant of a sitting president, Omar Hassan al-Bashir of Sudan).

Tony Blair–(1953-) Former Prime Minister, at Tubingen University in Germany 2000: "You can say that globalization started here in Germany, with the fall of the Berlin Wall and the end of the Cold War."

Pope John Paul II–(1920-2005) January 2004 … "with a renewed call for peace in the Middle East and Africa and the creation of a New World Order based on respect for the dignity of man and equality among the nations. This year he directed his thoughts to continuing conflicts around the globe. But he stressed that to bring about peace, there needs to be a new respect for international laws and the creation of a New International Order, based on the goals of the United Nations."

Kevin Rudd–(1957-) Australian Prime Minister, has "denounced the unfettered capitalism of the past three decades and has called for a new era of "Social Capitalism" in which government intervention and regulation are featured heavily," spoken at the United Nations in 2009.

Pope Benedict XVI–(1927-2022) "In the face of the unrelenting growth of global interdependence, there is a strongly felt need, even in the midst of a global recession for a reform of the United Nations organization, and likewise of economic institutions and international finance, so that the concept of the family of nations can acquire real teeth to manage the global economy; to revive economies hit by the crisis; to avoid any deterioration of the present crisis and the greater imbalances that would result; to bring about integral and timely disarmament, food security, and peace; to guarantee the protection of the environment and to regulate migration; for all this, there is urgent need for a true world political authority."

CONCLUSION

AT THE BEGINNING of this book I told you that you would have to think, decide, and make your own choices. I am not asking you to believe me or to side with my ideas. That would be a failure on both our parts. I do believe that you owe it to yourself to research and find your own answers for yourself. Though I have kept this book short and manageable it still carries a lot of nuggets for you to consider and think about. God is not a difficult or confusing God. He wants us to know and prepare ourselves or He would have never told us it was even possible.

The Bible clearly tells us that we have the potential to know. . . Whosoever. . . If we seek, we shall find. If we knock, the door will be opened. If we hunger and thirst for the truth, we shall be filled. If we lack wisdom, all we have to do is ask Him that gives it freely. And Blessed is those that read this book (Revelation or Bible) and understand it. All things are Possible with God.

APPENDIX A

MILLENNIAL WEEK

Sunday (1.) 1000 years	Monday (2.) 1000 years	Tuesday (3.) 1000 years	Wednesday (4.) 1000 years	Thursday (5.) 1000 years	Friday (6.) 1000 years	Saturday (7.) 1000 years
Patriarchs		**Abraham Era**		**Church age**		**Judgment**
(Methuselah, Enoch, Seth, etc) (Adamic and Noahide covenant)		(Kings, Judges, and Prophets) (Abrahamic and Mosaic covenant)		(Jewish and Gentiles covenant)		(The Great White Throne Judgment of God (lost) and the Judgment Sit of Christ (saved) - rewards and punishments of our works). (You will only be under one of the Judgments, depending on your position)
(Adam was created about 4004 BC and Abraham was born about 2004 BC- about 2000 years apart, human error factor of + or- within five years.)		(Abraham was born about 2004 BC and Jesus was born about 4 BC-2000 years apart, human error factor of + or- within five years.)		(Jesus was born about 4 BC, Christ was Crucified about 30 AD, at 33 ½ years old. There will be a gap between His birth and death. The start of the Church was at Pentecost about 30 AD and will be completed around 2030: about 2000 years apart, human error factor of + or- within five years.)		(a 1000 year reign will start, Lucifer and his cohorts will be bound)
(During this time period they lived between 250-970 years old.)		(During this time period they lived between 80-180 years.)		(During this time period we live at best a max of about 120 years, the average between 65-85 years.)		(Seventh day: Rested- complete, holy, & blessed.)
(First and second day: Separated light from darkness, possibly good and evil from chaos; day from night. Separated expanse of water and called it Heaven.)		(Third and fourth day: Waters and dry lands; vegetation, trees and plants. Sun, moon, and stars; times and seasons.)		(Fifth and sixth day: Fishes, Birds, beasts, insects, and livestock. Mankind- dominion, multiply, and be fruitful.)		

APPENDIX B

NEW TESTAMENT

MATTHEW 7:15-20 **Beware of false prophets,** which come to you in sheep's clothing, but inwardly they are **ravening wolves.** You shall **know them by their fruits...** Even so every good tree brings forth good fruit; but a **corrupt tree brings forth evil fruit.** A good tree cannot bring forth evil fruit, neither can a corrupt tree bring forth good fruit. Every tree that brings not forth good fruit is hewn down, and cast into the fire. Wherefore **by their fruit you shall know them.**

MATTHEW 13:37-42,49-50 He that sows the good seed is the Son of Man; The field is the world; the **good seed are the children of the kingdom;** but the **tares are the children of the wicked one;** The enemy that sowed them is the devil; the **harvest is the end of the world;** and the **reapers are the angels.** As therefore the **tares are gathered and burned in the fire;** so shall it be in the end of this world. The Son of Man shall send forth His angels, and they shall gather out of His kingdom all things that offend, and them which do iniquity; And shall **cast them into a furnace of fire;** there shall be **wailing and gnashing of teeth.** So shall it be at the end of the world: the angels shall come forth, and **sever the wicked from among the just,** And they **cast them into the furnace of fire:** there shall be **wailing and gnashing of teeth.**

ACTS 8:17-21 And it shall come to pass **in the last days**, says God, I will **pour out of My Spirit upon all flesh**: and your sons and daughters **shall prophesy**, and your young men **shall see visions**, and your old men **shall dream dreams**: And on servants and on My handmaidens **I will pour out in these days of My Spirit**; and they **shall prophesy**: And **I will show wonders in heaven above**, and **signs in the earth** beneath: <u>blood, and fire, and vapor of smoke</u>: The **sun shall be turned into darkness**, and the **moon into blood**, before that great and notable <u>Day of the Lord</u> come: And it shall come to pass, that whosoever shall **call on the name of the Lord shall be saved** (see **Joel 2:28-32**).

ROMANS 1:18-32 For the **Wrath of God** is reveled from heaven **against all ungodliness and unrighteousness** of men, who hold the truth in unrighteousness; Because that which **may be known of God is manifest in them**; for God has shown it to them. For the invisible things of Him from the creation of the world are clearly seen, being understand by the things that are made, even His eternal power and Godhead; so that they are **without excuse**: Because that, when they knew God, they glorified Him not as God, neither were thankful; but became **vain in their imaginations**, and their **foolish heart** was darkened. Professing themselves to be wise, they became fools, And changed the glory of the incorruptible God into an image made like to corruptible man, and to birds, and four footed beasts, and creeping things. Wherefore God also gave them up to **uncleanness through the lusts of their own hearts**, to **dishonor their own bodies** between themselves: Who changed the **truth of God into a lie**, and worshiped and **served the creature more than the Creator**, who is blessed for-ever. For this cause God gave **them up to vile affections**: for even their women did **change the natural use into that which is against nature**: And likewise also the men, leaving the **natural use of the woman, burned in their lust one toward another**; men with men working that which is unseemly, and receiving in themselves that recompense of their error which was meet. And even as they did not like to retain God in their knowledge, God gave **them over to a reprobate mind**, to do those things which are not convenient; Being **filled with all unrighteousness, fornication, wickedness, covetousness, mali-**

ciousness; full of envy, murder, debate, deceit, malignity; whisperers. Backbiters, haters of God, spiteful, proud, boasters, inventers of evil things, disobedient to parents, Without understanding, covenant breakers, without natural affection, implacable, unmerciful: Who knowing the judgment of God, that they which **commit such things are worthy of death**, not only do the same, but have **pleasure in them that do them**.

ROMANS 2:5-9 But after your **hardness and impenitent heart treasure up to yourself wrath** against the **day of wrath** and revelation of the righteous judgment of God; Who will **render to every man according to his deeds**: To them who by patient continuance in well doing seek for glory and honor and immortality, eternal life: But to them that are contentious, and do not obey the truth, but **obey unrighteousness, indignation and wrath, Tribulation and anguish**, upon every soul of man that **does evil**, of the Jew first, and also of the Gentile.

I CORINTHIANS 15:51-52 Behold, I show you a mystery; We **shall not all sleep**, but **shall all be changed**, In a moment, in the **twinkling of an eye**, at the **last trump**: for the **trumpet shall sound**, and the **dead shall be raised** incorruptible, and **we shall be changed**.

II CORINTHIANS 11:13-15 For such are **false apostles, deceitful workers**, transforming themselves into the apostles of Christ. And no marvel; for **Satan himself is transformed into an angel of light**. Therefore it is no great thing if his ministers also be transformed as the ministers of righteousness; whose end shall be according to their works.

I THESSALONIANS 4:15-17 For this we say to you by the word of the Lord, that we which are alive and remain to the coming of the Lord shall not prevent them which are asleep. For the **Lord Himself shall descend from heaven with a shout, with the voice of the archangel, and with the trump of God**: and the **dead in Christ shall rise first**: Then we which are alive and remain **shall be caught up together with them in the clouds**, to **meet the Lord in the air**: and so shall we ever be with the Lord.

II THESSALONIANS 2:3-4,6-12 Let no man deceive you by any means: for that day shall not come, except **there come a falling away first**, and that **man of sin be revealed**, the **son of perdition**; Who opposes and **exalts himself above all that is called God**, or that is worshiped; so that **he is as god sits in the temple of God, showing himself that he is god**… And now you know what withholds that he might be revealed in his time. For the **mystery of iniquity does already work**: only He who now restrains will do so until he is taken out of the way. And then shall that **wicked one be revealed**, whom the Lord shall consume with the spirit of His mouth, and shall destroy with the brightness of His coming: Even him, whose coming is after the **working of Satan with all power and signs and lying wonders**, And with **all deceivableness of unrighteousness** in them that perish; because **they received not the love of the truth, that they might be saved**. And for this cause **God shall send them strong delusion**, that they **should believe a lie**: That they **all might be damned who believed not the truth**, but had **pleasure in unrighteousness**.

I TIMOTHY 4:1-2 Now the **Spirit speaks expressly**, that in the **latter times some shall depart from the faith, giving heed to seducing spirits, and doctrines of devils**; Speaking **lies in hypocrisy**; having their **conscience seared** with a hot iron.

II TIMOTHY 3:1-6,8,12-13 This know also, that in the **last days perilous times shall come**. For men shall be **lovers of their own selves, covetous, boasters, proud, blasphemers, disobedient to parents, unthankful, unholy, unloving, truce breakers, false accusers, gossips, without self-control, despisers of those that are good, Traitors, reckless, conceited, lovers of pleasures more than lovers of God**; Having a form of godliness, but denying the power thereof: from such turn away. For of this sort are **they which creep into houses**, and **lead captive silly women laden with sins**, led away with **various lusts**,… **men of corrupt minds**, reprobate concerning the faith… Yea, and all that will live godly in Christ Jesus shall **suffer persecution. But evil men and seducers shall wax worse and worse, deceiving, and being deceived.**

II TIMOTHY 4:3-4 For the **time will come when they will not endure sound doctrine**; but after their **own lust shall they heap to themselves teachers, having itching ears**; And they shall **turn away their ears from the truth**, and shall be **turned to fables**.

II PETER 3:3, 7,10 Knowing this first, that there **shall come in the last days scoffers**, walking **after their own lusts**,... But the heavens and the earth, which are now, by the same word are kept in store, **reserved to fire against the Day of Judgment** and **perdition of ungodly men**... But the **Day of the Lord will come as a thief in the night**; in which the **heavens shall pass away with a great noise**, and the **elements shall melt with fervent heat**, the earth also and the works that are therein shall be **burned up**.

1 JOHN 2:18,22 Little children, it is the last time: and as you have heard that **antichrist shall come**, even **now are there many antichrists**; whereby we know that it is the last time... Who is **a liar but he that denies that Jesus is the Christ**? He is **antichrist, that denies the Father and the Son**.

1 JOHN 4:1-3 Beloved, **believe not every spirit**, but **try the spirits whether they are of God**: because many **false prophets are gone out into the world**. Hereby know you the Spirit of God: Every **spirit that confesses that Jesus Christ is come in the flesh is of God**: And every **spirit that confesses not that Jesus Christ is come in the flesh is not of God: and this is that spirit of antichrist**, whereof you have heard that it should come: and even now already **is it in the world**.

2 JOHN 7 For **many deceivers** are entered into the world, who confesses not that Jesus Christ is come in the flesh. This is a **deceiver** and an **antichrist**.

I have given you some food for thought. There are many more red flag, I hope you got the point. You the reader must decide for yourself with the evidence and proof, just how far do you think we are at in the Endtime Prophecies Amplified?

BIBLE REFERENCES

All-in-one, bible reference guide (2008). Grand Rapids, MI: Zondervan.

Apocrypha (2013). Grand Rapids, MI: Baker Publishing Group.

Holman Christian Standard Bible (2004). Nashville, TN: Holman Bible Publishers.

Holy Bible (RSV), Catholic Edition (2004). New York, NY: Oxford Press Inc.

Holy Scriptures, Tree of Life Version (2015). Grand Rapids, MI: Baker Publishing Group.

King James easy reading study bible (2001). Goodyear, AZ: G.E.M. Publishing.

King James Version (2001). Colorado Springs, CO: International Bible Society.

New American Standard Bible (1998). Anaheim, CA: Foundation Publications, Inc.

New Century Version (1991). Dallas, TX: Word Publishing.

New Living Translation (2013). Wheaton, IL: Tyndale House Publishers, Inc.

NIV/The Message Parallel Bible (2006). Grand Rapids, MI: Zondervan.

Quest Study Bible (NIV) (2003). Grand Rapids, MI: Zondervan.

Revised Standard Version (1971). Nashville, TN: Thomas Nelson, Inc.

The American Patriot's Bible (NKJV) (2009). Nashville TN: Thomas Nelson, Inc.

The Complete Jewish Study Bible (2016). Peabody, MA: Hendrickson Publishers Marketing.

The Everyday Life Bible (Amplified) (2006). New York, NY: Hachette Book Group.

The Founder's Bible (NASB) (2012). Newbury Park, CA: Shiloh Road Pub.

The New English Bible (1972). New York, NY: Oxford University Press.

The New King James version (1982). Nashville, TN: Thomas Nelson Publishing

The New Strong's Exhaustive Concordance of the Bible (1996). Nashville, TN: Thomas Nelson Pub.

Young's Analytical Concordance to the Bible (1983). Grand Rapids, MI: Wm. B. Eerdman's Publishing Co.

AUTHOR REFERENCES

Carlson, R. & Decker, E., (1994). *Fast facts on False Teachings.* Eugene, OR: Harvest House Publishers.

Cornish, R., (2005). *5 Minute Apologist.* Colorado Springs, CO: Navpress.

Duck, R.D. & Richards, L. (2006). *The Book of Revelation, the smart guide to the bible series.* Nashville, TN: Thomas Nelson, Inc.

Duck, R.D. & Richards, L. (2007). *The Book of Daniel, the smart guide to the bible series.* Nashville, TN: Thomas Nelson, Inc.

Duck, R.D., (2015). *God has spoken and we know it.* Noble, OK: Icon publishing group.

Duck, R.D., (1995). *On the Brink.* Lancaster, PA: Starburst, Inc.

Fraley, B., (2013). *Revival or Judgment?* Phoenix, AZ: Christian Life Outreach.

Ford, P.L., (2015). *New England Primer.* Dalton House, London: FB & c LTD.

Graham, B., (2010). *Storm Warning.* Nashville, TN: Thomas Nelson, Inc.

Hagee, J., (2013). Four Blood Moons. Brentwood, TN: Worthy Publishing.

Hagee, J., (2006). Jerusalem Countdown. Lake Mary, FL: Frontline Charisma Media/Charisma House.

Hindson, E., (2014). 15 Future Events that will Shake the World. Eugene, OR: Harvest House Publishers.

Hindson, E., Hindson, E., (1996), Final Signs, Eugene, OR: Harvest House Publishing

James, T., (2010). The Departure. Crane, MO: Defender Publishing.

Jefferson, T., (1902 reprint). The Jefferson Bible. St. Louis, MO: Thompson Publishing Co.

Jeremiah, D., (2008). What in the World is going on? Nashville, TN: Thomas Nelson Inc.

Jeremiah, D., (2010). The Coming Economic Armageddon. New York, NY: FaithWords Hachette Book Group.

Kuykendall, B.E., (1961). A comprehensive study of The Revelation. Athens, AL: Kuykendall's press.

Knight, G.W., (2001). A simplified Harmony of the Gospels. Nashville, TN: Holman Bible Publishers.

LaHaye, T., (2002). The Merciful God of Prophecy. New York, NY: Time Warner Company.

LaHaye, T. & Jenkins, J.B., (1999). Are we living in the End Times? Wheaton, IL: Tyndale House Publishers, Inc.

Lindsey, H., (1985). The Rapture. New York, NY: Bantam Books Inc.

Lindsey, H., (1973). Satan is alive and well on planet earth. Grand Rapids, MI: Zondervan Publishing House.

Rhodes, R., (2001). The End Times in Chronological Order. Eugene, OR: Harvest House Publishers.

Reaboi, D., (2010). Shariah: The Threat to America. Washington, DC: Center for Security Policy Press.

Salus, B., (2014). Nuclear Showdown in Iran. La Quinta, CA: Prophecy Depot Ministries.

Stone, P., (2011). Unleashing the Beast. Lake Mary, FL: FrontLine Charisma Media/Charisma House.

Stone, P., (2015). The Eight Kingdom. Lake Mary, FL: FrontLine Charisma Media/Charisma House.

Swindoll, C.R., (2010). The Church Awakening. New York, NY: FaithWords Hachette Book Group.

Yusuf, A.A., (2008). The Qur'an. Elmhurst, NY: Tahrike Tarsile Qur'an Inc.

Television, Radio or Internet sources:

Barton, D., Foundation of Freedom (TBN).

Barton, D. & T., www.Wallbuilders.com.

Batchelor, D., Amazing Facts (TBN).

Baxter, I., endtimesministries.com (Endtime Ministry, Daystar).

Jefferies, G., Bible Prophecies Revealed (TBN).

Jones, A., www. infowars.com.

Lindsey, H., The Hal Lindsey Report (TBN).

Morris, R., Robert Morris Ministries (TBN).

ABOUT THE AUTHOR

DAVID D. CEIGA was born in East Chicago Indiana in 1961. He graduated from Highland High School in 1980, and has retired from the U.S. Navy (1981–1996). He is married to his beautiful wife Sara since 1982. He has one son along with a step-daughter and a step-son. His family includes eleven grandchildren and ten great-grandchildren. Since 1997 he has resided in Union City, Tennessee where he has also retired from the Goodyear Tire and Rubber Company in 2011. He has an associate's degree in psychology from Midcontinent University and a bachelor's degree in social work with a minor in world religious from the University of Tennessee at Martin. In his spare time he enjoys studying various Biblical topics, US current events as well as US history. Dave is also an active member of his local church.